†HE GOSPEL OF CHRISTMAS

REFLECTIONS FOR ADVENT

PATTY KIRK

IVP Books

An imprint of InterVarsity Press
Downers Grove, Illinois

InterVarsity Press
P.O. Box 1400, Downers Grove, IL 60515-1426
World Wide Web: www.ivpress.com
E-mail: email@ivpress.com

*InterVarsity Press® is the book-publishing division of InterVarsity Christian Fellowship/USA®,
a movement of students and faculty active on campus at hundreds of universities, colleges and
schools of nursing in the United States of America, and a member movement of the International
Fellowship of Evangelical Students. For information about local and regional activities, write
Public Relations Dept., InterVarsity Christian Fellowship/USA, 6400 Schroeder Rd., P.O. Box
7895, Madison, WI 53707-7895, or visit the IVCF website at <www.intervarsity.org>.*

All Scripture quotations, unless otherwise indicated, are taken from THE HOLY BIBLE, NEW
INTERNATIONAL VERSION®, NIV® *Copyright © 1973, 1978, 1984, 2011 by Biblica, Inc.™
Used by permission. All rights reserved worldwide.*

Lyrics to "Sister Winter" from Sufjan Stevens, Songs for Christmas *(Asthmatic Kitty, 2006),
reprinted by permission. All rights reserved.*

"Faith of a Child" and "Joseph's Dreams" reprinted by permission. Confessions of an Amateur
Believer, *Patty Kirk, 2007, Thomas Nelson Inc., Nashville, Tennessee. All rights reserved.*

*While all stories in this book are true, some names and identifying information in this book
have been changed to protect the privacy of the individuals involved.*

Design: Cindy Kiple
Cover image: © peter zelei/iStockphoto

ISBN 978-0-8308-3785-4

Printed in the United States of America ∞

Library of Congress Cataloging-in-Publication Data

The gospel of Christmas: reflections for Advent / Patty Kirk.
    p. cm.
Includes bibliographical references.
ISBN 978-0-8308-3785-4 (pbk.: alk. paper)
1. Advent—Meditations. I. Title.
BV40.K565 2012
242'.332—dc23

2012018669

P	17	16	15	14	13	12	11	10	9	8	7	6	5	4	3	2	1
Y	26	25	24	23	22	21	20	19	18	17	16	15	14	13	12		

Contents

PREFACE

Ever since I became a Christian a dozen years ago, I have been gripped by the urge to write in the weeks before Christmas. Sometimes a phrase in a carol seizes me. Or I get to wondering about some intriguing aspect of the Christmas story—the idea that God himself passed through a human birth canal or that a mucky feed trough cradled his newborn body. Most Christmases, when I hear the account of the nativity read in church, I'm surprised by a detail that I never noticed before, even though I have studied the various passages closely for years.

This Christmas, I noticed that as the wise men were following the star, they were suddenly "overjoyed" (in my translation of the Bible) to see it. Their response seemed meaningful somehow—as if they had perhaps lost sight of the star for a while and were worried that it might have disappeared for good—and I wanted to write about it.

The Christmas mandates of our culture—shopping for presents, sending cards, making gingerbread houses and doing other elaborate Christmas crafts with my children—sometimes overwhelm me, and writing about them serves as an outlet for stress. Often, in the weeks leading up to Christmas, traumatic events of past Christmases revisit me and the jolliness of Christmas seems a burden. And so I write, and the resulting essays go into a computer file labeled "Advent."

The chapters in this book are taken from that Advent file. They are not the final word on the accounts of the birth of Jesus in the Bible, of course. I get some things wrong, I'm sure. I also read differently than a real theologian is likely to read—more speculatively, certainly, and more in the context of my own experience. In my view, God's coming to us in the form of a human baby, if it really is the good news the angel says it is, must be good and relevant not just to those shepherds who first heard it proclaimed but to me, today, in the world I live in. So I tell it that way: as not only God's story but also my own, the story of his advent into my life.

I

C⊙ⅢE

B efore I knew the meaning of the word *advent*—
before I ever read the word in a book or used it to refer
to the arrival of something new (the advent of an idea;
the advent of global warming, of global terrorism, of
world peace)—and certainly before I learned in my
high school Latin class to dissect the word etymologi-
cally into *ad-* (to) plus *venīre* (to come) to mean the
coming of God to our world as one of us, I knew what
advent was in the simple way children know things.
Advent was, in my Catholic childhood, the charged
month or so before Christmas.

It was a church word, of course, and had thus inherited all the heavy meaninglessness of such words,

which tended to run together with other church words in memorized prayers and stately turns of phrase that only make sense to me now in adulthood. It was like the word *bounty* in the blessing my family raced through before every meal: "Bless-us-O-Lord-for-these-thy-gifts-which-we-are-about-to-receive-through-thy-bounty-through-Christ-our-Lord-amen."[1] What child knows what *bounty* is—what the word signifies, what it really means—when she has never known want? To give thanks for bounty in childhood was like pledging allegiance to an indivisible republic. Even if I had known what those words meant—*pledging, allegiance, indivisible, republic*—I was not capable of conscious allegiance then, much less allegiance toward a body politic of which I was not yet a voting member and a unity whose opposite I couldn't imagine. I had not yet learned to appreciate these boons—unity, bounty, the coming of our Lord—the way we learn to appreciate most good things: by longing for them in their absence.

Advent back then, in any case, was more than merely the mysterious church word that produced the candles, three purple and one pink, in the Advent wreath an altar boy lit successively on each of the four Sundays before Christmas. And it was more than the traditional songs sung at that time of year— "O Come, O Come, Emmanuel," "Come, Thou Long Expected Jesus"—sad songs in my child ear that I was glad to replace as Christmas neared with happier carols like "Joy to the World, the Lord Is Come!"[2] Although I was a believer of sorts even in those days, when the words of faith meant little, Advent was not primarily a church matter at all but rather a name for the electric weeks between Thanksgiving and Christmas Day. Weeks of wondrous smells and sounds and visions. Cookies baking. Songs jingling everywhere you went. The glittery red cover of the Sears Christmas Catalog. Presents. Snow.

Advent was, first off, a time of longing for these future pleasures. A child yearns as at no other time in the days leading up to Christmas, and is perhaps more aware then than at any other time of the possibility of disappointment. *Maybe I won't get that rock tumbler,* I worried. *Or, worse, maybe one of my sisters will get it and I'll get something awful.* Contemplating the future is always a scary undertaking.

But then there were also the immediate delights, the sensual ecstasies going on right then, in the midst of all that longing. Early in Advent my sisters and brothers and I unpacked our family's dusty collection of gnomes and set them out in our living room. They were made of pine cones and frosted with glitter, with matted cotton ball beards and little pointed hats. I loved those gnomes. And the lights on the eaves. And even the homemade candy canes my dad made one year that turned out soft and droopy because he didn't cook them right. Another year I made stained-glass cookies from a recipe in a magazine. I cut patterns in sugar-cookie dough and put different colored Life Savers in the empty places, and after they melted they really did look like the windows of our church. I loved how our Christmas tree filled the house with its scent and how, when we moved to Connecticut, a rocky outcropping on the side of our

road always produced a crop of yellowish icicles sometime before Christmas.

Whenever the weather got cold enough to freeze the big
swamp near the center of town, my sisters and brothers and I
went skating. It was cold to the point of pain, and the weedy ice
was really too bumpy to skate on, but these miseries were small
payment for the thermos of hot chocolate our parents sent
along with us. Almost as much as I enjoyed my share, drunk
tandem with my sisters from the thermos's aluminum lid, I enjoyed knowing it was there while I lurched around on the ice—
hot, sweet, waiting for us. I loved, in short, the sheer excitement
of that time of year, when my consciousness evolved from wanting to having, from imagining to seeing, from guessing to
knowing. For me as a child, Advent was the best time of the
year. Primarily for that reason, the birth of Jesus was the best
news ever.

The concept of Advent has been popularized since my childhood. Many families I know these days have some sort of Advent calendar on their refrigerator with paper doors that open
to expose a toy or treat or, for the more devout, a religious image
or Bible verse for every day leading up to Christmas. Teachers
use Advent calendars at school—entirely secularized, of
course—as a fun way to teach children about scheduling and
the number of days in a month and the passage of time. My
mother-in-law has an Advent calendar made of green felt with
numbered pockets holding stuffed Christmas symbols—a
Christmas tree, a teddy bear, a candle and so on. From baby-

hood my daughters have taken turns pulling out the object in the next pocket and, with great ceremony, attaching it by its Velcro tab to the accompanying felt Christmas tree.

Strangely, the churches I've attended since becoming a believer as an adult don't usually celebrate Advent to speak of. Some don't even use the word. For me, though, the word *Advent* still shimmers, has always shimmered, with the significance it had for me as a child. In my nonbelieving years of early adulthood, when God's coming meant nothing to me and Jesus was just a story people told to dispel their fears about death, the weeks before Christmas nevertheless crippled me with longing. I didn't know what I longed for anymore. I was past presents, past hoping, past the days when icicles and snow and colored cookies constituted bliss. And yet, throughout Advent I longed anyway, in my various lonely apartments. Secretly. Silently. Hotly.

Nowadays when I take notice of the word as Christmas approaches, when I read it somewhere or hear it or form its parts in my mouth—*ad-* and *-vent*—when it occurs to me that Advent has arrived and God has come, I feel the longing and satisfaction of a lifetime coalescing to a single urge within me. Come. Come. O come!

The coming of God to us echoes with the mandate to come to him in response. Jesus often tells those around him to come.

"Come, follow me," he says to Simon and Andrew, "and I will send you out to fish for people" (Matthew 4:19; Mark 1:17).

To the "harassed and helpless" crowds (Matthew 9:36) who perpetually follow after him he says, "Come to me, all you who are weary and burdened, and I will give you rest" (Matthew 11:28).

"Let the little children come to me," he tells those of his followers who want to keep kids from bothering him (Matthew 19:14; Mark 10:14).

"Come to the wedding banquet," he says in the voice of the exultant king in his parable, who wants to celebrate his son's marriage (Matthew 22:4).

"Come and share your master's happiness!" he says in another parable, this time in the voice of the master to those of his servants who have made wise use of the wealth he left in their hands (Matthew 25:21, 23).

"Zacchaeus, come down immediately. I must stay at your house today," Jesus tells the despised little tax collector, who has climbed a tree to get a look at him over the crowd (Luke 19:5).

And he tells the rich man who has kept all the commandments since he was a boy, "Go, sell everything you have and give to the poor. . . . Then come, follow me" (Mark 10:21).

"Come out of him!" he commands the demons, again and again (Mark 1:25; Luke 4:35).

"Lazarus, come out!" he tells his dead friend, already starting to smell bad in his tomb (John 11:43).

"Come," he tells Peter simply, when the disciple threatens to leave the boat to make sure it's really Jesus out there in the darkness before dawn, coming to them across the water (Matthew 14:29).

Those who do come often repeat Jesus' command to others. "Come, see a man who told me everything I ever did," the

Samaritan woman at the well tells the people of her town. "Could this be the Messiah?" (John 4:29). Similarly the disciple Philip, immediately upon answering Jesus' call to follow him, tells his friend Nathanael, "We have found the one Moses wrote about in the Law" (John 1:45). When Nathanael balks, claiming that nothing good ever came out of Nazareth, Philip says, "Come and see" (John 1:46).

Answering the call to come in Scripture almost always results in faith. When Jesus raises a widow's son from death, his followers and a large crowd of mourners from the woman's town not only believe Jesus is a great prophet and are filled with awe but, in their astonishment, unwittingly proclaim the good news of Christmas: "God has come to help his people" (Luke 7:16). God has come.

This news is the crux of my faith—the glad tidings of great joy the angel proclaimed to the shepherds. The *adventus Dei* of my Latin class: the coming of God to his people. Advent. The gospel in a word.

Because of Advent, I came. I come still. And you will come too, I hope. And eventually, through God's coming, his children will all come—back to the cradle, back home, back to where we belong.

2

THE FIRST
SNOW OF WINTER

The announcement of an Advent chapel at the Christian university where I teach English always lures me in with the promise of carol singing and pine smells and Christmassy stories of generations of longing fulfilled in the birth of a child. I love Advent. I love that it is a time to think about presents, promises, happy memories and good things to come—usually arriving, for me, after a long period of stress, spiritual penury and emotional malfunction.

This year's Advent chapel opened with a choral rendition of Amy Grant's haunting song about Mary, in which God's own mother-to-be faces her usually ignored but probably accurate confusion and worry about the Spirit-conceived, out-of-wedlock child growing inside her and begs the "Breath of Heaven" to hold her together and be forever near her.[1] It was the perfect place to start my ideal Advent chapel, capturing the almost-despair, almost-faithlessness of those for whom hope has not quite arrived, for whom even the promises of better things to come are so far in the past that they are caked in layer upon layer of doubt.

As the choir sang, and particularly as the lead singer mouthed the song's prayer chorus, I thought of Mary's plight, which is so often our plight in life as well. Scared. Entering miseries she never dreamed would come upon her. Excited but also burdened by her pregnancy, the marriage to Joseph and the impending birth. Struggling with relationships—with her husband, her parents, her friends and relatives. Traveling to another town when she didn't feel so great. Soon to flee widespread infanticide at the hands of Herod. The lead singer repeated her prayer for the Breath of Heaven to hold her together, to stay forever near her, and the singer's strong but hesitant and worried-sounding voice really did remind me of an adolescent Mary.

Here's what Advent is about, I thought, *this need and darkness and worry. And far beneath the ashen misery, heavy confusion and doubt are the faint red glimmers of excitement and hope.* Advent, the period leading up to the birth of the Messiah—which for Mary would correspond to the last month of her pregnancy—is a time when emotions compete with one another. Anticipation. Fear. Confidence. Misgiving.

Maybe it's possible to find happiness in all of this, I imagined Mary thinking as the plaintive song ended. *A betrothal that almost ended in divorce. Carrying a child when I'm a virgin. Maybe it's possible that this baby boy—that my love for him—will be strong and wonderful enough to outweigh all the accusations and indignities I will suffer on his behalf. Maybe God's promises are true and he hasn't forgotten his creation. Maybe he really does love us, loves me in particular, even me.*

But as the Advent chapel continued, the carols to celebrate the fulfillment of Mary's hopes never came. I am like my daughters—and many of my students, I find, though I don't usually share their taste in worship music—in my desire for jolly traditional carols during the Christmas season. Charlotte and Lulu want nothing new, nothing in a minor key, nothing they have not sung every Christmas of their lives. Christmas songs are like the ornaments we take out of their dusty boxes to decorate the tree: loved for their familiarity and the happy times they symbolize more than for their intrinsic beauty or theological correctness.

The Advent chapel that day was all about theological correctness. We sang the doleful "O Come, O Come, Emmanuel," which Charlotte and Lulu hate and I remember hating when I was young.[2] Nowadays I like it. Having sung it every Advent of my Catholic childhood, the hating of it has become an essential part of the season. In the original Latin text, which dates from the twelfth century and is based on an even older Advent prayer, its message is still in the "Breath of Heaven" mode: a prayer for deliverance from such miseries as ignorance, darkness, quarrels and death. In John Neale's familiar English translation, the lyrics become even darker, begging God to ransom Israel from "lonely exile," "the depths of hell" and "Satan's tyranny"—a faith-filled wish, certainly, but hardly the cheerful Christmas affirmation that captive Israel's prayer for deliverance had been heard and hope was on its way.

After "O Come, O Come" came, comically, a surprisingly fierce "What Child Is This?"[3] followed by a procession of contemporary worship songs that were decidedly un-Christmassy. None of the traditional carols, of course. My evangelical peers have deemed most of these "unbiblical," with their snowy scenes and Latinisms and wise men arriving on Jesus' actual birthday instead of weeks, months or even years later, when Jesus and his parents were no longer camping out in a stable. Some of the songs we sang during the Advent service even mentioned the suffering and crucifixion of Jesus and his subsequent resurrection—chronological errors and violations of Aristotle's dramatic unities of time, place and action, to my mind,[4] in addition to being a party-pooping way of celebrating Jesus' coming.

It depressed me. I know we're supposed to get happy about the crucifixion. After all, without it there can be no resurrection. No empty tomb without the dead body, as it were. To be totally honest, though, let me just say that the resurrection has never filled me with the elation I experience when I consider the incarnation of God himself as a human baby: the emptying, the stooping, the kneeling down to our level—in the manner of the good kind of adults when interacting with children—that is the birth of God in human form.

It may be that my Catholic upbringing is at issue here. In the churches of my childhood, the torture, death and burial of Jesus—referred to as the Passion and depicted in bas-relief Stations of the Cross (in Latin the *Via Dolorosa*, or "Road of Suffering") around the walls of every Catholic church—are a source of misery and pain. Catholics often cry when they pray the rosary around the Stations of the Cross during Lent. Famous Catholic visionaries who connect with God in special ways often do so through experiences of pain and sorrow. They witness tears on statues of Mary. They cry themselves. They bleed from their hands and feet and sides. They are burdened by the suffering of God's Son, not ecstatic about it. Though they anticipate the resurrection joyfully on Palm Sunday, lacing the floor of the church with palm leaves and singing festive songs appropriate to Jesus' triumphal entry into Jerusalem just before his death, the celebration of Easter itself is often a subdued affair. Not like Christmas.

Or maybe it's like Christmas at midmorning, when you're surrounded by the mess of wrapping paper and sweaters and shirts in plastic bags and half-eaten candy. The kids, who got up way too early, are starting to squabble and get hungry, but you don't really want to cook bacon and eggs because you're tired and cranky, too, and in an hour or so you'll be packing up to go to your in-laws' house to eat turkey and cornbread stuffing and mashed potatoes and thick white gravy—in the middle of the day!—and open more presents and get happy all over again. The realization of the promise—of a Savior, of eternal life—is meaningful only in the context of the suffering and want that precede it. And the ecstasy of fulfillment, for me, is a fleeting thing, sweetest in its anticipation, in our fantasies of happy families and children's wish lists and snow.

It snowed last night. The first snow of winter. It is the tenth of December. Lulu is on day three of the flu. Two nights ago she asked me if people really could die from the flu, as she had read that very young children and the elderly had been doing in Colorado, Texas and, more recently, Oklahoma, where we live.

"Yes," I told her, "but you won't die."

I make these sorts of promises all the time. And so far, luckily, all my promises have come true. For reasons I have never understood, Lulu has always been maniacally worried about matters of health. When I get sick, she is certain I will die, and her worry for her own health plays itself out in fierce denial of even the most obvious symptoms of illness.

"I am *not* sick," she used to say as a toddler, just as she was throwing up all over the front of my nightgown. Even now, at fourteen, she will not allow anyone to take her temperature, gets angry if I suggest she take some Tylenol or even hand her a tissue, refuses every suggestion that we take her to the doctor, and insists on attending school even with a fever or when, convinced that her sickness is about to turn into nausea, she hasn't eaten for a couple of days. She likes to believe that things are as they should be, that she is happy and well and wants for nothing, and that if she ignores any evidence to the contrary these blessings will continue eternally.

So last night when it snowed, Lulu—cough, stuffy nose, fever and all—was out there in it and left a message on the snow-padded picnic table for me to find this morning. Nothing esoteric. Nothing everyone has not at some time or another scratched on a rock high up on a hillside or spray-painted on an overpass or carved into a tree. "LULU WAS HERE." And beside it, because it was snow, because it was the amazing substance it is, weird and wet and cold and malleable, and because it was there, she made her handprint.

This, to me, is what Advent is about. In the midst of the bleak reality of our mild Oklahoma winters, in spite of illnesses that confine us to the house and parents who try to stick thermometers in our ears, in the dark of night and behind the backs of the mean-minded ones who claim to be in charge of the elements, despite meteorologists and grandparents predicting lovely sunny weather throughout the month of December, my daughters' ardent hope that sometime around Christmas, ideally before, it will snow.

That's it. Just that.

And then it will snow, and we will make frenetic angels in it and throw balls of it at our moms and pack pretend sweaters of it onto our wagging dogs and eat it with maple syrup and cream and shape it into roly-poly men with jagged smiles.

Days later it will be dirty, and the dogs will have peed on it, and puddles will appear in the low places, and all that will be left is the eternal memory of how wonderful it was for that wish to be fulfilled. And that wish will stay with us, unremembered, through the wet black spring and the sweaty summer and the sycamore-smelling fall, until the days start getting dark in the afternoon and hot baths and steamy drinks are a comfort and everyone's nose is running.

And then it will fill us with longing, and we will remember what we knew, and we will think, *Well, it did snow that one winter, and it's winter, and, well, it* could *snow.* And we will listen more closely to the weather news and talk about it.

"They said it was going to snow."

"Probably not much. Just a skiff, that man on channel five said."

"But still."

And then suddenly there's a cold breath of night air rushing in through the open door and the dogs are barking and someone has remembered to turn on the Christmas lights on the porch and the girls are getting mad because they can't find their gloves because it's here, it's here, it's Christmas, it's snowing!

3

ADVENT

One of my yearly frustrations at Christmastime is the inevitable series of sermons and complaints from church, family, friends and even strangers whose opinions shape public sentiment through the popular media that the trappings of Christmas, the frantic shopping and present exchanging and piles of hollied catalogs, the jingle-belling of the Christmas season, have nothing to do with what Christmas is really about: the incarnation of God in the person of Jesus.

Now, many characteristics of Jesus' physical entry into our world move me. Like all naturally birthed human babies, he was discharged in great pain by his human mother and emerged, as each of us once did, a humble mystery: purplish of skin, scrunch-faced from the pressures of birth, and probably screaming upon his arrival from the pain and shock of it. He was a real baby born of a real woman, in a real place—although certainly humbler than most—a real stable somewhere, redolent of manure and the steamy breath of domesticated animals, a temporary home unwillingly proffered and shared with chattel and food sources, creatures even humbler than humans.

Mary's story particularly touches me. She is, first off, so quietly faithful and accepting in her response to the angel's announcement. "I am the Lord's servant," she tells him. "May your word to me be fulfilled" (Luke 1:38). What is the essential difference between this teenager and me that made her willing where I would certainly have balked? Upon learning of the shepherds' experience and later her young son's astonishing eloquence among the teachers in the temple, Mary, Luke tells us twice, "treasured up all these things and pondered them in her heart" (Luke 2:19 and, worded slightly differently, Luke 2:51). Mary's apparent habits of reasoning and reflection, coupled with her obedience to God's will, are the exact combination of traits to which I aspire as a believer.

What impresses me most about Mary, though, is the frailty of even *her* faith. One would think that she, of all believers in the world, would have found faith easy. After all, she not only knew Jesus throughout his life on earth and requested miracles of him and saw them fulfilled, but she was visited by an angel and overshadowed by the Most High. She bore God's Son in her own body. Even so she struggled as a believer. Despite incontrovertible proofs of the reality of Jesus' deity, she resisted what she knew to be true, as I see it, when she and her other sons tried to wrest their crazed family member from his followers in order to protect him. Knowing what she did about God's involvement in Jesus' life from conception onward, how could she later think God was not in control of what happened to him? I find considerable reassurance in Mary's apparent doubt, just as I do in Peter's denials and in Thomas's need to put his fingers in Jesus' wounds. Evidently, God expects little from us as believers. It is enough to treasure up a lifetime of experiences of God and ponder them. Or, as the writer of Hebrews says, to *hope* them into faith. That too is an essential mystery of the story of the birth of the baby God.

Then there are the generations of longing that preceded the nativity, longing begot of misery and terror but also of the vague promises of prophets despised until they were dead, promises whose most compelling feature was their redundancy. There would be a Savior more powerful than Moses or David, a king wiser than Solomon, a leader more holy than any of the prophets, a way out of the wretchedness of the Israelites' history, a hope beyond any they could imagine for themselves. What amazing mysteries! The hope of centuries—realized in a willing virgin girl, a puling baby, a smelly barn.

And yet it irks me when, sometime before Thanksgiving or maybe even Halloween, someone close to me makes the inevitable sour remark about lights going up on certain houses known for their yearly display or the shelves at Walmart filling up with singing Santas and glitter-encrusted ornaments and the newest style of tinsel.

"Can't they at least wait until after Thanksgiving?" someone will whine. It's always someone I love and otherwise respect, my husband or my mother-in-law or one of my friends. *Who are these ones who can't wait until the allotted time?* I muse on their behalf. *Are they the unsaved? Are all storeowners and light-lovers lost?* Meanwhile, someone else sourly confirms the original objection with the appropriate learned response: "Well, they just want to show off." Or, "They just want to make a buck."

And then, during Christmas season proper, the lectures condemning the celebrations of the heathen begin in earnest. We are reminded of the *real* reason for the season and the falsity of all commercial expressions of it. The stern reminders of what it's really about creep into even the music we play in church; biblically accurate hymns like "O Little Town of Bethlehem" house the message directly and eschew anything that hints at what the lost world is caught up in: the mad excitement, the jostling impatience, the sheer crazy joy of Christmas. Among the majority of my current crowd of friends, to send a jolly snowman greeting card amounts to an endorsement of Satan and his minions as well as the world of commerce, whose irreverent language we otherwise embrace and proliferate in every aspect of our lives.

Every season I feel obliged to hide my own excitement when, before Thanksgiving and sometimes even Halloween, the

weather turns cold suddenly and my daughters get out our
Christmas CDs and newspaper ads and radio announcers start
mentioning upcoming productions of the *Nutcracker.* Secretly,
because it seems to run so counter to what my loved ones keep
telling me, I anticipate this time of year keenly—the gingerbread house my daughters and I will build and the prospect of
snow and new ornaments for the tree. I am especially excited
about the wild enthusiasm of nonbelievers, if that's what they
are. The hopeful light displays of the benighted. The Christmas crowds at the mall. My greedy daughters' ardent desires for
the presents that are promised them, independent of their good
behavior, every Christmas morning.

My family's actual celebrating begins with those first CDs.
The girls' favorites are Bing Crosby's *White Christmas*[1] and *A
Christmas in Europe,* a collection of choral hymns—familiar carols,
but sung mostly in languages Charlotte and Lulu can't understand—by the Pueri Cantores (Singing Children) of Merano.[2]
I prefer Amy Grant's *Home for Christmas,*[3] even though since her
divorce Grant has been persona non grata among my mostly
conservative Christian acquaintances. I play our choices over
and over again on the CD player in the kitchen while I cook the
soups and pumpkin bread and persimmon cookies of fall. "It's
beginning to look a lot like Christmas," I sing along, swaying.
"*In dulci jubilo!*"[4] Along with my daughters, I'm already dreaming
of a white Christmas.

In Amy Grant's songs especially the pagan excitement and
the meaning of Christmas seem to collide, as the dancing cou-

ples do in their attempts to get under the mistletoe in "Rockin'
Around the Christmas Tree."[5] And my favorite Christmas song
of all invites, "O come, all ye faithful, joyful and triumphant! O
come, all ye citizens of heaven above."[6] In October I am already
sobbing to this song, whether it's Bing or Amy or the Pueri
Cantores of Merano singing. It is a call to worship if there ever
was one, a hymn to my unholy impatience for the event of the
season. Oh come! Let's go! Bring it on!

My family and I watch *How the Grinch Stole Christmas*[7] and
Home Alone[8] and *A Charlie Brown Christmas*,[9] all of which share the
theme of selflessness. Although *Home Alone* features a church
crèche and Linus recites the Christmas story from Luke—the
old-fashioned phrasing and mature-sounding words of King
James's time are especially touching in his artless child voice—
little else in these movies even alludes to what the season really
brings: God in the form of a human child.

Every Christmas season my husband reads aloud from an
anthology called *Treasury of Christmas Stories*. It's a cheap paper-
back Scholastic book now long out of print that Kris has had
since he was a child and probably bought through the public
schools. He reads one story a night. The book's brown pages are
crumbling at the edges and its binding is broken. Every year we
have to shuffle the pages around a bit when we first get it out,
and every year I remind myself to get on the Internet and find
a used copy in better condition.

The stories and poems in the *Treasury* are decidedly secular.
No mention of Jesus or Mary or yearning Jews here. There's

"'Twas the Night before Christmas"[10] as well as the chapter titled "Mr. Edwards Meets Santa Claus" from *Little House on the Prairie*, in which poor Laura and Mary get excited about their presents of a tin cup, a stick of peppermint, a penny and a little cake made with white sugar for each of them.[11] There's also the story of a boy who wants to get his dying mother a rosemary plant[12] and one in which a girl gets her wish to have Christmas all the time and soon gets sick of it.[13]

But my family's favorites are two stories about children wanting horses for Christmas. One is the heart-wrenching story of a boy whose parents pretend on Christmas morning to have given him exactly what he said he wanted if he couldn't have a horse: nothing at all. The horse they actually bought him is delivered later in the day, as he sits on the front stoop crying.[14] The other story is a poem called "Secret in the Barn" by Anne Wood.[15]

It is Wood's poem I look forward to most at Christmastime, even though it exasperates my daughters whenever my husband reads it aloud because I cry so much. In it, the speaker, a little girl named Louise, has asked for a horse for Christmas, and she can't go to sleep on Christmas Eve because of her anticipation that she might really be getting one. So her mother plays a game with her in which they take turns imagining what everyone is doing who has to work the next day—nurses and train engineers and people up on utility poles. Even though we're at home for Christmas and having fun, the mother gently reminds Louise, people still get sick and "every blessed Christmas Eve" the phone or electricity goes out and someone has to go out in the cold to fix it.

Underneath this pious game of thinking of others before oneself—the seemingly inevitable theme of all Christmas fictions, which really does shape the poem—is the live current of Louise's impatience for that horse. The electric energy of longing and remembered promises. The exciting evidence—the snorting, champing horse noises out in the barn—that what she longs for and what she gets are about to coincide, as they so infrequently do, in the amazing mystery of Christmas. In some sense, Louise longs for what we all long for, even if we have never been interested in horses. Something warm, noisy, lovable, alive. Something that belongs entirely to us. Something so far beyond our deepest fantasies it seems the product of longing itself.

It embarrasses me to say it, but I look forward to "Secret in the Barn" more than I do a reading of the real Christmas story, even Linus's rendition of it (although that too makes me cry). In the retrospection of my faith, Wood's poem brings home to me what the season really means more emphatically than the words of the prophecy-examining Matthew or the orderly doctor Luke or even Jesus' best friend John. It is this: that the best of all worlds, what we hardly dare hope for in our ignorance and benightedness and impatience, *really did happen.* On a specific day in the past. Through the writhing exertions of a genuine woman who submitted to God's weird plan. In a real barn in the real town of Bethlehem. Witnessed by a confused but faithful husband and real donkeys and cattle and dazed shepherds and incandescent angels. "Secret in the Barn" reminds me of what happened and continues to happen in every believer since that day: the incarnation of God in human flesh.

That, for me, is the secret in the barn: the event that even those who don't yet know it to be true nevertheless long for, as ardently as Louise longs for her horse. The secret in the barn is what nonbelievers unwittingly anticipate and instinctively begin to celebrate long in advance of its scheduled anniversary. It positively delights me that even atheists, believers of other faiths and—those most lost of all—retailers, ignorant or unconscious of or even antagonistic toward the reason for the season, can't help but commemorate the birth of God's Son in their parties and presents and candles in the window. They peer out into the darkness, searching, like little hopeful Louise, for the impossible evidence of something they can't clearly see. And their hearts beat faster when they hear, or think they hear, that faint whinny of hope.

Maybe something's really out there, they unknowingly yearn as they stuff another holly garland into the shopping cart or pencil through their lists of how happiness might be achieved this year. Smelling the scents of Douglas fir and gingerbread baking in the oven, of fresh manure and hay and blood, they must unconsciously recognize the promise evident in all creation—as Paul tells us they do in Romans—and they must long for it. And for one long moment, anticipated long in advance of propriety and good taste, they join in the celebration of those who already know the secret. "O come, all ye faithful," they hum along in the aisles of Costco. In that moment, ecstatic as we all are then, we don't even notice that they're there among us, the hungry ones who still long for what we have already secured for ourselves. The reason for the season. The truth behind it all.

What has Jesus to do with bells and snow and Dr. Seuss's Whos holding hands singing reverent-sounding gibberish, you ask? The collision of hope and longing and delight in the reality of someone—the long expected one—arriving. Someone as merry and fragrant and real as a newborn baby, a better present than we could ever have dreamed up for ourselves. Hanging a wreath on the door, a bit of mistletoe from the lintel, we can hear—if we listen—someone's out there, in that charged moment of almost arrival, stomping around in the cold and blowing on his fingers, about to be with us, about to be ours.

Any woman who has ever anticipated a birth will tell you this: There is no other joy like it; nothing even comes close. Even though pregnancy can be fraught with worry and impatience, even though it brings with it responsibilities and pain and perhaps money problems, it is nevertheless the happiest time of her life, and somehow even strangers pick up on her excitement. When I was pregnant, passing acquaintances would suddenly strike up a conversation about the baby or even press their hands, as if in longing for *my* baby, on my hard belly. I received shower gifts from people whose names I didn't even recognize. Their enthusiasm, I know, was not for a child not their own. Many who celebrated my pregnant state would never even see or know my child. Rather they were drawn by the mystery and promise of life within me and the contagious thrill of awaiting its coming.

4

THE FAITH
OF A CHILD

Unlike most of the people I go to church with these days, I wasn't always much of a believer. As a child I attended church weekly and did believe in God, but I never heard about concepts like having a "personal relationship" with Christ or giving my troubles to Jesus. My relationship with Jesus Christ was respectful but remote, like my relationships with relatives I knew only from my parents' stories. As I was growing up, my troubles took me not into the arms of God but ever further from the faith of my childhood, and I spent much of my adult life unable to believe at all.

I grew up one of six kids in a Catholic family. I was baptized not long after I was born, and we attended church every Sunday, where I listened to three readings from the Bible: one from the Old Testament, one from the Epistles and one from the Gospels. I made my first communion when I was six or seven. At twelve I was confirmed in my faith by reciting my baptismal vows and adding the name of a saint to my other names.

Polycarp. I had to fight the nuns and get permission from our monsignor to use a male name. I chose Polycarp, I explained to Msgr. Dziodosz, not just because his feast day was my birthday but because I liked his story in our family's *Little Pictorial Lives of Saints.* Faced with martyrdom unless he cursed Christ, Polycarp replied, "Eighty-six years I have served Him, and He never did me wrong; how can I blaspheme my King and Saviour?"[1] In my child mind Polycarp was saying, "Well, I've followed God for so long that it hardly seems worthwhile to change now." The strange pragmatism of this statement of faith struck me as funny.

My family ate fish sticks on Fridays, and we carried in our station wagon a cross-shaped wooden box that twisted open to reveal a bottle of holy water, a white silk stole and a rolled-up sheet of paper with instructions on how to perform an emergency baptism. Sometimes when my parents drove us places I fantasized about coming upon an accident and watching my father crouch beside a dying person to read the words on the paper, getting spots of blood on the stole.

This was in the sixties, before the modernizations of the

Second Vatican Council had really sunk in. In those days my sisters and I wore organdy dresses poufed out with stiff slips to church and bobby-pinned lace caps to the tops of our heads. My older sister Sharon told funny stories about the nuns at a parochial school she had attended for a while. I coveted a soft-focus painting of Jesus praying that night in Gethsemane that Sharon had above her bed—the sky the inkiest midnight blue above what I thought of as the cheery lights of Bethlehem twinkling below.

My dad told stories too. Of stealing the communion wine in his altar boy days. Of a gigantic nun who punished him by lifting him off the ground by that especially tender hair that grows at the temple. Of his uncles shouting, "Jaysus, Mary and Joseph!" Of snow and knickerbockers and growing up in Brooklyn, which were all part of my Catholic heritage, as it seemed to me.

On Christmas Eve some years my parents took us to midnight Mass. Imagine it. You're six or seven or eight years old and have never stayed up past nine o'clock, not for any reason, and certainly not on Christmas Eve—that night of nights when presents appear out of nowhere and the air itself quivers with carols. You were so excited when they put you to bed that you couldn't sleep for a long time, but now, seconds later it seems, your parents get you and your siblings up out of the warm covers and thrust you into your church clothes. Nobody talks much. It is the middle of the middle of the night, and the world is darker and quieter than it has ever been in your remembrance. And then you're riding in the back of the station wagon, and then you're in the cold church, waiting.

Your mother or father gives your siblings and you each a little candle from a box at the end of the pew. It has a paper apron around it that your mother whispers is there to protect your hand from drips of wax. And then the lights go out, and the whole church is dark except for a leafy crèche at the altar: a Hawaiian-looking house surrounded by palm fronds. And you sit in the dark, waiting.

Soon there is a shuffling noise from behind, and you crane around to see. First some altar boys appear, some of them your age or even younger, carrying gigantic candles on poles. Behind them the priests come swinging censers wafting the exotic smoke of frankincense and myrrh. It is a fabulous smell that collects in your nose and sinks to your lowest places and stays there. Days later your closet will smell of that night.

The priests wear white vestments and Christmas-colored stoles, and the monsignor has on his magenta hat with the pom-pom, and they all look old fashioned, somehow, like Santa Clauses from an ancient book. Then your father or your mother lights your candle and your sisters' and brothers' candles, and then the whole church is filled with the glow and smell of candles burning, and everyone sits in the unfamiliar light and the silence and waits. Finally, the priest starts the Mass, and you sing carols, and everyone files past the crèche for communion.

At that time I knew this about God: He was real. Although he lived in heaven, he was everywhere too. He knew me and heard me and could see me every moment of the day. He could see into my very thoughts. He had a Son who was born in a Hawaiian-looking house surrounded by farm animals and shepherds and his mother and father. The Son was real too. Even though he was later killed on a cross, he came alive again and then went to heaven, where he still is, and he knew me just as his Father did. And because of this the ghost of him lived in me, and someday I would die and go to heaven where God and Jesus were and live there with them forever.

My faith as a child was, in other words, not much different from my evangelical Christian faith now. I believed in God and in his Son, in his Son's death and resurrection, and in my own resulting salvation from death. I wasn't very clear on the idea of sin, it's true, but I knew God loved me enough to forgive me and others for whatever we did wrong. I believed in the Father, the Son and the Holy Spirit. I believed in eternal life.

In the intervening years, as an atheist, I married a Christian, and he told me that this faith of my Catholic childhood was enough for him, even though I had abandoned it—or, as I felt, it had abandoned me. My childhood faith was enough, in fact, for God himself, this silly little man who married me told me. "Once saved, always saved," he said—which, he explained to me, meant it wasn't possible to lose true faith in God. It was a new concept for me. But I knew he was wrong. The faint glimmer of the faith I had once had was not enough to fill me with the light of genuine belief. That much I knew. And without faith, I was not saved. I was not a Catholic. Not a Christian. Not going to heaven or anywhere else when I died, no matter what anyone told me. And there was nothing I could do about it.

Faith, I somehow intuited, must come from outside of me. It must come from God himself, if it was true at all. And it didn't come, so it must not be true. That was my atheism.

Now, though, looking back, I wonder if my husband was right. Perhaps, even as a child, I did believe enough to be clutched back to the bosom of God had I lain me down to sleep one night and died. Perhaps if I had died some more realistic death—from a disease like the one that killed my mother or in an accident—perhaps even in those later years when I no longer felt loved or heard or even noticed by God, when my prayers disappeared into the black vacuum of night and I knew no one was listening, perhaps even then I would have survived death because of the almost forgotten faith of my childhood.

But for years, my husband's absurd assurance that I believed, no matter what I thought, amused me. I knew what I knew. Or what I didn't know. And even years later, when I became a believer again, it seemed to be not from sin that I was saved but from that black night of my inability to believe. Not from hell and death but from the conviction that I was *not* seen or known or heard when I prayed, that I was *not* loved by God.

My years of atheism made such an impression on me—the hope I hid from my friends, the longing for something beyond what I saw around me, my complete inability to pray—that I often forget now about the faith of my childhood. And it may be merely a vestige of that child's worldview, made up of presents and nighttime ceremonies and the familiar Christmas decorations we took out of dusty boxes every year and arranged on the mantle, but the crux of Christianity for me has never been the cross. Not then, not now. Instead it is God's first response to our hope and longing and frustrating blindness: the birth of his own Son in our world. What matters most to me is that God had that Son to begin with. And that he has other sons and daughters like me whom he loves and doesn't want to be parted from. That he loves his children as I love my own daughters—only more so, with a hot, knowing, parental love that says, "Be who you are, but love me back. Only love me back."

I wear a certain necklace a lot, a silver baby on a chain. People I know at school and church and sometimes even strangers come up to me and ask me what it means.

"Are you showing that you're against abortion?" they ask me.

So I explain that no, it's not an aborted baby but a baby Jesus. I prefer wearing the baby Jesus to wearing a cross, I tell them.

If it's around Christmastime, they usually nod approvingly. But if it's Eastertime, I usually have to say a bit more. Actually the baby is a Mardi Gras king-cake baby that I bought in New Orleans, a detail which could complicate my explanation because of the association of Mardi Gras with Lent and thus Easter, but I don't ever try to explain any of that.

Sometimes I consider this exchange an important opportunity to correct the macabre habit my fellow evangelicals have of bringing the crucifixion into every discussion of who God is, even discussions of the birth of Jesus. At my church's Christmas sing-along, someone invariably requests "Up from the

Grave He Arose"[2] or "Redeemed by the Blood of the Lamb!"[3] Wearing the silver baby pendant is my attempt to get them to see the ghoulishness of such thinking.

But the bigger ministry of my little necklace is to me. Hanging from that chain is not the baby Jesus at all, but me, one of God's daughters. A cherished daughter who once knew him a long time ago and who, without thinking about it much, simply loved him back, as children do. A wayward daughter to whom he revealed himself almost from her birth but who nevertheless ran from him and refused to love him back, despite the almost constant evidences of his enduring love and protection. I am, mysteriously, God's own baby girl. One of many children whom the Father sent his Son into our burning world to carry home to him.

One year during midnight Mass, when the dark was suddenly lit up with candles and we were waiting in the blaze for the Mass to begin, my baby brother, Tim, yelled into the holy silence, "And now everybody sing 'Happy Birthday' to me!"

The silence deepened for a second or two with my family's embarrassment, then Msgr. Dziodosz boomed from the altar his deep laughter. Exactly like Santa Claus. And then everyone else laughed too.

5

"Stille Nacht"

The other day, my friend Carli was describing her deep friendship with one of her cousins, a woman her same age who is about to get married. They grew up together, switching off staying at each other's houses for weeks at a time, and even as adults they share many common interests. Both love to read. Both ended up being lawyers. Both became Christians.

"We have had a lot of the same experiences," Carli concluded, "so I know her better than I know any other friend. We understand each other. Like Mary and Elizabeth."

It has always impressed her, Carli said, that God— having first challenged Mary's faith with a virgin pregnancy as well as the prospect of giving birth to and raising God's Son and the probable repercussions of these developments in her personal life—immediately thereafter helped her believe by providing someone like Elizabeth.

"Blessed are you among women, and blessed is the child you will bear!" Mary's much older relative exclaims as soon as she sees Mary at her door. "But why am I so favored, that the mother of my Lord should come to me?" (Luke 1:42-43). Elizabeth instantly recognizes and validates the moral rightness of what should look all wrong: the out-of-wedlock pregnancy of the betrothed younger woman.

Elizabeth understands Mary's situation because she is in similar circumstances herself. Not only is she too miraculously pregnant—six months along in an old-age pregnancy also announced by the angel Gabriel—but the baby in her womb "leaped for joy" when Elizabeth heard Mary's greeting at the door (Luke 1:44).

What sounds so prophetic in the text, the fetal John's womb-leaping response to Mary's arrival, is, in fact, the most common of miracles, something every pregnant woman has experienced. My babies leapt and kicked and rolled and somersaulted in my womb all the time. Charlotte surged like a whale within me whenever Kris and I ate banana splits, my passion during that pregnancy. And in my subsequent pregnancy, if I exerted myself in any way—to get up out of bed or run to answer the phone—Lulu was as squirmy as a trout.

But Elizabeth—although she has surely run to the door to

greet Mary and perhaps just finished a big bowl of pistachio ice cream—understands the movement of the fetus in her body to be prophetic. Filled with the Holy Spirit, she utters the first Hail Mary, confirming in her bodily experience and her enthusiastic words the very experiences and words that Mary herself must have been struggling to process and accept, even though she was willing to go along with God's plan. Impossible births. Angel visits. Resulting relationship problems. The mockery of the community. That God provided Mary with such a friend as Elizabeth amounts to, for my friend Carli, one of his most precious promises to his children: In our loneliest and most confusing moments, he will send companions who understand us and can see past the immediate crisis to the truths that might be found there.

It strikes me that crises are often catalysts for loneliness. Faced with trouble or a significant quandary, faced with fear, we often feel alone in the midst of it all. I felt this way for an entire year after a sexual assault that occurred in my twenties. Although I was surrounded by friends, each one wanting to help and support me in my suffering, a deep loneliness took hold of me. No one could really understand my situation, I was sure, and so I retreated into my aloneness, exiled myself to it, just as, when my husband and I used to raise cattle, a sick cow would go off from the herd and hide herself in a thicket of trees. I felt not just alone but, paradoxically, forsaken.

I was a nonbeliever during my years of loneliness, without any consciousness of God's presence, but even people confident in their faith often feel lonely when enduring anguish. My friend and colleague Carrie Oliver, an enviably devout and upbeat Christian woman who struggled with pancreatic cancer for two years before she finally passed away in 2007, described this loneliness in an online journal she kept in the last two years of her life:

> What is surprising are the incredible lonely moments that come like waves. Loneliness is different than fear, or sadness, or depression, or anxiety. It is defined in the dictionary as: being without the company of human beings, it means being cut off from others. Let me assure you I am not cut off from others. I have precious friends calling, coming over, going places with me, sending me notes and so much more. I have people I don't know sending me notes. But something about cancer says, "I am different than you" and that puts me somewhere where you are not. . . . If we are honest, that is what we feel when we get lonely. We feel different and cut off.[1]

Carrie felt this way, even though she was surrounded by people who loved her. Indeed, she had so many friends and family and well-wishers that, reading her journal and its accompanying guestbook, I often felt embarrassed by my own scanty acquaintances. *Who will accompany me on that sad journey one day?* I wondered. I know far fewer will mourn me when I am gone.

In the midst of Carrie's abiding loneliness—and perhaps because of it, as my friend Carli believes—she frequently met someone else undergoing a similar struggle, usually another patient in one of the countless waiting rooms she visited or someone who had come across her online journal and e-mailed her. A stranger, in other words, suffering in secret, also confused and afraid, also alone. In her journal, Carrie prayed for these new acquaintances and urged her readers to do the same, and she surely considered her interaction with them and intercession on their behalf to be important ministries. But these exchanges clearly benefited Carrie as well. She took deep comfort and vital companionship from their shared experience. Rereading Carrie's fervent accounts of these fleeting visitors to her life, I think my friend Carli may be onto something in seeing God's hand in such meetings. It is as if, although he allows our suffering, he doesn't want to abandon us to the loneliness of having to sort through it on our own.

Loneliness, I have always thought, is a winter emotion. In my favorite poem, Rainer Maria Rilke's "Herbsttag" ("Fall Day"), the speaker describes the end of the harvest season and the slow onset of winter as a time to write long letters and wander alone in the streets.[2] If you haven't yet found a house, you won't build one now, the speaker tells us, and if you are alone, you will remain so for a long time. "Herbsttag" is an ode to loneliness and encapsulates in its images and phrases exactly the feelings I had, often for months on end, in the years I lived abroad. I was never actually by myself in the cities to which I fled after my assault. I made friends wherever I went and often spent time in their company. But in my memories of those years, I am always alone. In my cavernous apartment in Berlin eating a bowl of the soup I had been eating for every meal for a week. Staring out at the empty gray afternoon from my concrete balcony in Beijing. Winding a meaningless path through the crowded streets of Kowloon, seeing what there was to discover, utterly alone in a thicket of strangers. I was cut off culturally and linguistically from those around me, but it was not just that. My loneliness was constitutive. It became who I was. Separate. Quiet. Still.

The poem that for me describes those years of loneliness should sound forlorn, I suppose, but it doesn't. More than anything else, Rilke's "Herbsttag" communicates autumn. Ripe fruit. Sweet, heavy wine. Leaves scattering in the wind. Paradoxically, a key word in the poem is *Vollendung*, a word that connotes happy completion or accomplishment, literally a "full ending." It is the consummation of a season—or a day or a life—well lived.

I have thought a lot about Carli's notion that God provides for the lonely. It is not the first time I have thought about loneliness in the context of faith. Years ago a group of women at my university asked me to mentor them. I was flattered and agreed to do it, although I was sure that the mentoring would probably be the other way around. I was a relatively new Christian in those days and felt out of my depth in matters of faith. They, by contrast, were all lifelong believers and almost scarily devout. They spoke of God's will in their lives as though it were a set plan, right down to the courses they took and the friends they made and whether or not they should get another part-time job or borrow more money to pay for school.

All of them were single and desirous of being in a committed relationship, and they sought evidence of God's views on singleness and marriage in all sorts of biblical places. They worried about being "unequally yoked" and questioned me closely about my own marriage, which had come about despite the fact that Kris was an ardent believer and I was an atheist when we met. One of them had recently stopped seeing a guy she had been dating for years because, she said sadly, he didn't share her faith. Another believed all dating was "unbiblical," and the others tried to convince her this wasn't so. They spoke again and again of their hopes of getting married and wondered how proactive they should be in finding a mate. All agreed that God would provide the husband they were meant to marry. If he didn't, they said, they would remain single. They talked about the struggles of singleness, about how they were treated differently at church than their married friends, about how articles on singleness in Christian magazines got it all wrong.

This was new territory for me. I didn't read such magazines and wasn't familiar enough with their world to understand their views and complaints. I didn't know what to tell them, what counsel to offer the lonely from my own lonely, godless, pre-marriage years, so I searched the Christian world in which I found myself—their world—for some sort of foothold.

It seemed to be the habit among educated Christians, I found, to present singleness in a positive light. A speaker in chapel preached that some are "called" to singleness, and most of my colleagues offered students the same advice I had grown up with: Get your education first, then marry. One should be content in one's singleness, everyone seemed to be saying from all directions. This message frustrated the women in my little group. They said it was as if people were determined to convince them that they shouldn't long to be married, as they all did.

One of the women in the group had interrupted her studies to work as a missionary in Korea for a while and was in her thirties. She pointed out that in Genesis, having just created the world and everything in it and declared it all good, God said, "It is not good for the man to be alone" (Genesis 2:18). Aloneness, in other words, is *not* good, she said. So God provides companions. Lovers. Spouses.

And children, I added silently. And their teenage friends. Neighbors. Colleagues. Enemies. Salespeople in the entryway of every store at the mall offering to help you. Total strangers calling you daily to offer things you don't want. E-mail spam. The noise and activity of others wherever you go. There is no escape from this provision of antidotes to being alone, it seems to me, and during our discussions I often envied these women their singleness. When I look back from the frenzy of my life as a wife and mother to the years of my life when I too was lonely, I have the fiercest experience of longing.

The women in the group were busy too, though, they said. They had roommates and classes and jobs and church activities and so many friends that they too often felt overwhelmed by the demands on them. Even so, to a woman, they wished there were someone present in their lives on a daily basis.

"Someone who cares about my schedule," one of them said.

"Someone to sit next to at church," another added.

Someone, in short, who was there all the time and who, of necessity, paid attention to the same preoccupations—large and small—that make up a life.

I remembered feeling the same desire when I was their age—although for them a committed relationship meant marriage, whereas for me, in the days of my loneliness, it merely meant a guy who wanted to be together with just me. I wanted to wake up beside the same person in bed every day, someone I wanted to talk with at breakfast, someone I could cook for, someone who cared what I put in my shopping cart at the grocery store.

When I finally did marry Kris, I was—and I still am— deeply appreciative of these and other joys of marriage and how they anchored my life. That said, even early in our marriage I secretly—and sometimes not so secretly—longed to be left alone, if just for a moment. To think. To write. To eat a solitary meal. To take a walk. To inhale the winter air and examine the stout little plants able to withstand the cold—kale, collards, turnips—that were just then emerging from the dirt of my garden and lifting their seeds up above them. To not worry about where Kris was and how he and I would coordinate our efforts to pick up the car at the shop. To not know, not care, which daughter needed to go where and when.

But it wasn't just relief from busyness and responsibilities I longed for, I told the students I mentored. Something about marriage seems to obliterate aloneness and leave you no space to speculate and consider. Barely room even to dream or yearn—as they all did, as I had done in their circumstances. Very soon in my relationship, I told them, the business of belonging began to consume who I was. Or, perhaps, to put it another way, I got so caught up in the details of our shared existence—the schedule, the car, the children, the 10:50 church service—that I no longer paid much attention to the real events of my life, no longer pondered their meaning or treasured them up in my heart.

Did Mary feel the same way sometimes? I wonder now. Did she long for a quiet place in the tumult of giving birth and fleeing to Egypt and finding a cheap place to live and making friends among strangers and wanting to be home? And then, back home again, was she teased by her best friends for that early birth? "So devout, this out-of-wedlock mom!" she might have overheard someone in the synagogue say. She would have been alert to such comments, conscious of others' disdain. Did Mary yearn to escape the wonderful plan she had become part of: God's provision of companionship—Immanuel, God With Us—to the entire world? As she was raising up Jesus and soon his brothers and sisters, as she reviewed their activities in her head so she wouldn't forget one, as she washed clothes with the other women of the town and helped organize a niece's wedding, did she, like me, long to escape the commotion, the words spoken and not spoken, the noise and responsibility and turmoil of belonging, the "with-ness" of life, and just be alone?

Alone. This is a word I dream about sometimes. When I said as much to the women I mentored, I could tell it annoyed them. I'm sure they thought I was doing what we Christians are always doing to the singles in our midst. Counseling them to "just wait for God's timing" and enjoy their singleness while they still could. Telling them only how frenzied marriage is and nothing about its joys. Trying to convince them that, contrary to God's own pronouncement on the subject, to be alone is a *good* thing. And, in the process, relegating them to their singleness.

The other day I brought my friend Edda a loaf of bread. Edda lives alone and loves my bread. My favorite sourdough recipe—for the bread of Puglia, which has a chewy crust, a wet crumb, and big, uneven holes—doesn't really work unless you make a big batch, so I always make three loaves and give away one or two. As soon as I presented the bread—the loaf hadn't even made it from my hand to Edda's—she was already telling me exactly what she was going to eat with it that night. She had some shrimp, she said, and was planning to sauté them Greek-style with lemon juice and basil, cut-up tomatoes and lots of garlic, and the bread would be just perfect to sop up the juices.

In my mind I saw it all—in a flash of fantasy so charged with longing it miraculously converted the week-old soups of my years of aloneness into feasts for one. I saw the plate on the table. The six pink shrimp in their pool of fragrant olive oil. The book I was reading propped against the butter dish. The glass of piny, yellow retsina that Edda, a teetotaler, wouldn't be drinking but that I certainly would. Faintly, behind me somewhere, the *tick tick tick* of a clock on the wall. And except for that ticking, the blessed, blessed stillness of the room.

Stillness, strangely, is a word that comes up a lot in connection with the Christmas story. Jesus' birth night, like any other nativity, was surely a hectic event—perhaps even more hectic than most, occurring as it did in a shelter intended for animals—but nevertheless it's often represented as "still." Think Christmas-card depictions of the Mother and Child and the German carol *"Stille Nacht,"* which we know as "Silent Night." The *stille* of the song's original title is not incorrectly translated as "silent" in the English translation, but the German word conveys—as does our word *still,* which we inherited from our language's German roots—the blessed elimination of not only noise but movement, the absence of all sensory evidence of others who want to talk to us or attract our attention or engage us in some activity.

Christmas mornings at my house are anything but silent or tranquil. Even now, as teenagers who make precise lists of what they want for Christmas and thus know in advance the likely contents of every wrapped package under the tree, my daughters still pounce on my husband and me in our bed while it's yet dark out and demand that we get up—*Right now!*—and go downstairs to the living room where everything is in disarray, a visual commotion of colors and shapes and blinking tree lights.

An argument—by now an essential tradition of Christmas morning—ensues about whether Mama should get her coffee before or after the presents are opened. Kris wins and I get my coffee, but not without raucous exertion on all sides.

Then there's the tearing of paper and the trying out of the new electronic noisemakers in the household and Kris's patient wadding of trash into the slithery black bag we stuff alongside the piano. Before long it's time to head to Mamaw's house, a quarter of a mile down the road, for ham and biscuits and more present opening and trying on of clothes. Our dogs lead the way there, barking and leaping back and forth in front of the car as we drive, as if celebrating, frolicking, as if they too know it's Christmas. And then Mamaw—who is in her eighties and has for years been in denial about the fact that she needs a hearing aid—is bellowing her hellos and wanting to assemble us all in front of her Christmas tree for a picture and shouting questions about sizes and fits, and we are all moving and shouting too, explaining what she misunderstands and repeating our answers, each time louder.

Sometime in it all, we are home again and there's a lull. The girls disappear into their rooms, and Kris and I nap on our bed, and the stillness I have been longing for all morning—for all of Advent, for all my life—is finally upon me. But I can't rest. I am thinking of tonight, the next meal, the rest of the mess downstairs. Of how much money we spent and shouldn't have spent, of my yearly trip to Dallas to see an old friend and how we will afford it.

Kris is asleep beside me, his breathing as regular and light as a baby's. This is his greatest spiritual gift, I think. The ability to sleep when I can't. He sleeps the sleep of a child, the sleep of the truly faithful. He embraces the stillness.

My friend Carli's revelation about Mary and Elizabeth's relationship came to her as a teenager, when she read a fictional account of Mary's life called *Two from Galilee*.[3] The part of the book that impressed her the most, she said, was that it made plain to her for the first time what it meant to long for the Messiah. Even though it's the essence of Advent, this longing, we struggle to understand it, now that the Messiah has already arrived. It's hard to enter the minds and hearts of a people who didn't yet have what we often forget to enjoy: a God who became like us and shared our most human experiences—our loneliness, our confusion, our pain. The closest I can get to the Israelites' centuries of longing—their inherited yearning for a comfort like no other that they looked forward to and yet, having never known it, could not quite understand—is my own hunger for stillness, for a place to be alone in the midst of my hectic life, for true and lasting rest.

Rest is a remedy frequently promised in Scripture. "Come to me, all you who are weary and burdened," Jesus pledges directly in one such promise, "and I will give you rest" (Matthew 11:28). In more than one passage, Jesus himself seems to be our promised rest. Elsewhere "rest" appears to mean arriving where you need to be, and in many passages it is synonymous with death.

I prefer to think of rest, though, as exactly that: rest. Respite from activity and worry and noise. Sleep. The quiet, trusting sleep of my husband when all is well with him. The sleep of Jesus in the boat while his disciples shrieked that they were going to drown. The sleep of Stephen. The sleep of Moses and Abraham and Rahab the prostitute and all the other famous believers mentioned in Hebrews who, although predating the Messiah by many generations, nonetheless believed in God's promise of salvation and awaited the day when they would be united with him—with us!—in paradise.

In the tumult of Moses' difficult leadership of God's people, at a moment when he is confused and uncertain about what God wants of him and so upset with his charges for making the golden calf that he has broken the tablets on which were inscribed the Ten Commandments, he confronts God:

> You have been telling me, "Lead these people," but you have not let me know whom you will send with me. You have said, "I know you by name and you have found favor with me." If you are pleased with me, teach me your ways so I may know you and continue to find favor with you. Remember that this nation is your people. (Exodus 33:12-13)

Moses' confusion and distress are palpable here. "You have said!" he repeats, and he reminds the All-Knowing of his responsibility to look after the Israelites.

Beneath Moses' anxiety we can hear his aloneness: *Aren't you sending anyone with me?* he wants to know. The Lord immediately assures him, "My Presence will go with you, and I will give you rest" (Exodus 33:14), but Moses can't hear these promises. His distress is too extreme, his worries too noisy, his loneliness too convincing for presence or rest to seem possible. "If your Presence does not go with us," he wails on, "do not send us up from here. How will anyone know that you are pleased with me and with your people unless you go with us? What else will distinguish me and your people from all the other people on the face of the earth?" (Exodus 33:15-16).

In the end God has to reassure him again and again—with more promises, a new set of tablets, and finally, in response to Moses' demand, a demonstration of his glory. Only after this last proof that God will not abandon him is Moses calmed—and calmed so completely that "when he came out and told the Israelites what he had been commanded, they saw that his face was radiant" (Exodus 34:34-35).

"Be still, and know that I am God," the Lord Almighty—our Father—tells us in Psalm 46, a calming liturgical hymn probably sung by the temple choir as they led believers to worship. The psalmist confidently concludes—as if in the radiant voice of Moses, reassured, and with all the confidence of Isaiah proclaiming Immanuel, God With Us, to be the name of the virgin's baby centuries before his birth—"The LORD Almighty is with us" (Psalm 46:10-11).

Presence. Rest. It is hard sometimes, so hard, to believe such promises. So hard to get to that stillness. I think, *Make me still. Still me, dear Father, as we still our children.*

In German, the verb form of *still* means to nurse a baby. To stop up its mouth, to relax its frantic grasping, with the comfort and warmth and nourishment of the nipple. That is my prayer during Advent, the gift I long for most. *Still my mouth, my hands, my schedule of activities. Make me like a newborn child—like your own Son on that first Christmas morning. I am incapable of stilling myself. Still me. Still my heart and the innermost writhings of my brain. Comfort me with your presence. Make me know I am yours.*

6

Joseph's Dreams

If we read the narrative of Jesus' birth from the perspective of Joseph, his earthly father, it is hardly a story of unmitigated joy. If we view it as fiction, though—as some Bible scholars claim it is, constructed after the fact for theological purposes—it seems a rather funny story, in a grim sort of way.

Imagine: You're in love with the sweetest, nicest, best-looking and most morally upright girl of all the girls in Nazareth, and even your parents agree that you two were meant for each other. So you get betrothed, and everything is going fine. You've got a steady job, she's eager to start a family, and you're just about to get married when she turns up pregnant by somebody else.

"It's okay," she reassures you, as if bad weren't bad enough. "I haven't been sleeping around. Honest. I mean, an angel came and visited me and told me God himself is the father. I'm serious. I didn't do anything wrong. He overshadowed me. I don't even remember it. If the angel hadn't told me it had happened, I wouldn't even know."

She tells you the baby's name, Jesus, a name that never was in your family or hers, probably the new boyfriend's dad or something. Worst of all, instead of being shamefaced or even glum about any of this, she's positively ecstatic. She even makes up a song about how wonderful God is and how his Son will be a king who will bring down the high-up and raise up the low-down, that he will be, in short, the Savior everyone's been waiting for.

Fine thoughts, you're thinking. God has made her pregnant. Yeah, right. And she looks for all the world like she's telling the truth when she sings this, but when you tell your two best buddies, they make jokes about her chastity and your stupidity.

So, not only is your girlfriend pregnant by someone else, but she's obviously deranged. How else could she say such things and act like she's telling God's truth? But you don't really have the heart to make a big deal about it. You've heard of women being stoned to death for less. A messy way to die that would surely reflect badly on you. And anyway, that would be punishing her for being crazy. Because you still love her, and even though you feel betrayed, you can't bring yourself to believe she's lying.

So, you start looking around for a lawyer or a rabbi or some-one who can undo the betrothal papers without a big to-do so that you two can go your own ways. It takes a few days to figure out how the thing is done. They never taught you anything in your Bible study class about how to get *unbetrothed*. You don't even know what to call it.

Meanwhile, Mary goes off to visit her cousin Elizabeth, an old lady who also just came up pregnant and is making all sorts of strange claims about *her* baby. It seems this brand of craziness runs in Mary's family. The cousin's husband, a really good guy in everyone's opinion, is so embarrassed about the whole thing with Elizabeth getting pregnant and saying such things that he hasn't said a word since. And you're like, this is too weird.

So, anyway, you just about have an arrangement lined up with this guy who makes his living divorcing people. He doesn't have a word for undoing a betrothal either, but he says it can be done. Then Mary comes back from her cousin's and you tell her how it's going to be, and she seems sad but grateful not to have to be stoned. But you haven't quite gotten up the guts to per-form the emotional suicide of telling your parents.

Mom has already ordered the wedding announcements and so forth. She invites you to supper, a prenuptial celebration such as she's been putting on every weekend since the betrothal. You plan it out: *Tonight I will tell them.* You rehearse it. At dinner, you drink more wine than usual, getting ready, and at one point you're just about to say, "Listen up! I have something to tell you." But at that precise moment, someone raises the inevitable toast—"Mazel tov!"—and your courage fails you. The words froth up, like some foul burp, and you end up going to bed having said nothing.

That night you dream, of course, about Mary and angels and God fathering human babies. You dream that you are naming the baby, that God has told you to name the baby Jesus, and you are raising him up like a glass of wine, someone else's son—"Mazel tov!"—and announcing his name to your assembled family. Someone is singing crazily, and this big brawny angel with hairy arms is lifting his glass too, saying something about the baby saving people from their sins and fulfilling various prophecies. Mazel tov.

Or perhaps it wasn't that way at all. Most of the details are missing, unfortunately, and we're left to surmise—as we usually are with ancient texts, especially biblical ones—much of what actually went on. Or perhaps, as those Bible scholars argue, the whole story is made up to house the prophecies the tax collector Matthew wanted to get across to his audience. Well, here's what we know from the text: Mary was pregnant and must have told Joseph something about it that made him want to divorce her quietly. Then he had a dream in which an angel reassured him that everything Mary must have said was true.

The part I struggle with is that dream. Or, rather, that Joseph believed his dreams to be messages from God. There end up being four more of these dreams that all come at crucial decision-making moments in Joseph's struggle to be God's earthly father, and I always wonder, were his dreams different from other people's dreams? Or could it be that *all* dreams are God talking to us, after a fashion, if we just had Joseph's faith?

I have dreams every night in which all sorts of people do and say all sorts of weird things, and I never regard them as direct communications from God. Once, I even had what I now regard as a prophetic dream, given that the event it seemed to be about really did come to pass at about the same time the dream occurred. But I've always explained the dream away as, at best, a paranormal glitch of sorts, a bulging of the supernatural realm into the natural one we live in. Or, at worst, an intriguing coincidence.

The regular dreams I have, though, seem to share a certain chaotic resistance to clean explication. How could God be talking to me if the message is so messy? How did Joseph unravel his dreams such that he knew what to do?

Just about every morning I take one or two of my dreams down to the breakfast table for my husband to interpret. It seems to me that each new dream has exactly the same basic elements as the ones the day before. Their main characters are almost always changelings, starting out as one of my family members from the past—my mom or dad or one of my siblings—and then metamorphosing into my husband or one of my students or a merging of one of my daughters into a son I never had. There are always urgent ideas, strong emotions such as fear or frustration or pleasure, and remembered events or fragments of speech recognizable from a day or two before.

Typically, patterns of problems repeat and occasionally resolve themselves. The apparent storyline of one part of the dream is told again with different characters or a slightly different outcome, as if to say, "Here, try this out." Or, "How about this?"

My dreams are, in brief, rather like the visions of Revelation: full of emergencies and repetitions and weird composite creatures. In both my dreams and John's visions, otherwise inauspicious objects or themes recur in episode after episode and acquire symbolic relevance. A house, my teeth, animals, making a phone call, bowls, lamps, deserts, remembered places where I've never been. Most dream interpreters these days, like Freud and Daniel and the Old Testament Joseph before them, appear to think my dream symbols mean the same thing as everyone else's, that there is a collective dream vocabulary—teeth are one's sense of self-worth, branches or baskets are days, men on horses one's impending death—translations as blithe and useless as hieroglyphics to the modern dreamer.

At the breakfast table, Kris, with that frightening efficiency of the innocent, cuts right through it all—symbols, characters, emotions—to find direct representations of what he thinks are the things currently bothering me in my life. His interpretations are often instructive but usually reveal more about what's bothering *him* than what my dream might actually mean. Our conversation goes something like this:

"Babe, I had this dream in which my sister Sharon brings a cat to our house, only it isn't really our house now but a house in Pompeii where, in my dream, we have been living for a while.

In my dream, you are a farmer again, and I am always making bread. But anyway, you bring in this cat you found on the road—because my sister changes into you—and it has gashes in it you want me to sew up. So, after I spend a long time not finding first a needle and then thread, I eventually manage to start sewing, but the cat turns out to be dead. Actually, I know that it was never alive to begin with, but nothing I can say will make you believe it. You are my sister again, and you keep saying, 'No, it's alive. You're just saying that.'"

Kris is making the coffee and, it seems to me, ignoring what I'm saying the whole time. I'm just about to say so when he says, "Your sister is my mom, and you think she shouldn't drive the girls to Siloam this Sunday when we're in Tulsa."

"But what does that have to do with my dream?" I whine. And he explains: The cat is the children, dead or about to be dead, and the Sharon-person who changes into him is his mom. And what he tells me has nothing to do with my dream, but he is so certain of his interpretation that I know he's really worried about the kids being driven by his mom. So, after we're finished talking, I call up Mamaw and tell her we don't want the girls to go to Siloam with her to her sister's house after all, and can't Uncle Dean and Aunt Lorraine just drive here and eat at her house?

Here's the thing. Joseph went at his dreams in a totally different way. He must have; otherwise, he would never have been so certain about what they meant. He went to bed worried—about marrying a pregnant woman, about taking care of a baby the king was trying to kill, about whether he should stay in Egypt or go back home, about where home was now that he'd been away for so long—and he woke up with a purpose and the certainty that his purpose was divinely inspired.

I'm thinking Joseph had no special gift of interpretation but merely an analytical method a lot more intentionally faithful than mine. He didn't ask Mary at the breakfast table or consult a dream dictionary. Instead, he stared right though the re-assembled chaos of his dream to his hopes buried there: that his wife-to-be was speaking the truth, that there would indeed be a Messiah, that God would protect him, that he had a true home, that his descendants would take possession of his ene-mies' cities, and that the boy he would raise as his son, God's Son, would be blessed by all the nations of the earth. He chose to see hope in his dreams instead of fears and to believe his hope to be true. Isn't that what the writer of Hebrews 11:1 tells us faith *is*, "confidence in what we hope for"—so sure that we can go forth without fear—"and assurance about what we do not see," even God's invisible qualities, which tend to get hid-den under the mess?

How did Joseph understand that God had spoken to him? He sifted through his worries to find confirmation of that most essential promise: the promise that, incomprehensibly, he mat-tered to God and would have a role in displaying God's glory. Joseph peered into his dreams for the message that he—a nobody, a carpenter from the podunk town of Nazareth—was called to be the lover of God's own choice in a woman and the protector of his infant Son. He accepted his dreams, like everything else in his life, as evidence that there was a hope worth waiting for, a future worth buying into, a love worth risking one's life and very sanity to believe in.

Don't misunderstand me. If anyone needed a visit from an angel, it seems to me, it was Joseph. And I know I've wished for as much myself to solve the petty miseries of my own life. What Joseph's story tells us, though, is that we matter to God. We are visited by angels nightly, but, unlike Joseph, we ignore them.

We matter to God. Inexplicably. Undeservedly. Even we dedicated Christians tend to forget this truth—or doubt it or reject it altogether—when we encounter trouble. It is difficult to understand why we matter, but we do. God is watching, listening to us, speaking promises into the cacophony of our worries and the certainty of their fulfillment into our most deeply buried hopes. To have faith, as Joseph did, all we have to do is pay attention as hope refracts what we see to reveal the future God has planned for his children. Faith means literally believing that in all things, even the crappiest ones, God works for the good of those who love him.

7

And He Is in
the Manger Now

❧

Prepare yourself: I am about to blaspheme. The divine mystery I am contemplating this Christmas is that God needs us.

Now, before you start getting all hot under your clerical collar, let me first say that I know God is all-powerful, all-present, all-knowing and all-sufficient. He is mightier than any concept of power our word *mighty* can encompass. His authority dashes any we may claim.

That said, Scripture attests again and again to God's desiring what he does not get from us. True mercy toward one another, not petty fulfillment of rules (Hosea 6:6). Cheerful giving to those with nothing, not mere exchanging of presents (2 Corinthians 9:6-11). Genuine love of those who hate us, not just conviviality with our friends and least objectionable relatives (Luke 6:27-36).

A friend of mine understands loving our enemies to mean actually liking those whom we most despise, an unrealistic demand on God's part if there ever was one but thoroughly comprehensible if we consider the kind of sibling love we long to see exhibited by our own children. We want them not merely to "love one another"—whatever that may mean in the context of sibling rivalry—but to get along, to play happily together, to think of their siblings as friends. In Noah's time, God longed so extremely for his children's love and decency to one another that, when it turned out the earth was "filled with violence because of them" (Genesis 6:13), he "regretted that he had made human beings on the earth, and his heart was deeply troubled" (Genesis 6:6). The original edition of the New International Version reads, "The Lord was grieved that he had made man on the earth, and his heart was filled with pain." God's attitude toward us, in short, is one of longing. Like the father modeled after him in Jesus' story about those rotten prodigal sons, God our Father stands at the gate searching the horizon for our return. And, so often, we don't return. Such unfulfilled longing, I would argue, presupposes need.

Which may be why—bear with me—God enters our world, our very consciousness as humans, in the very neediest of states: unequipped with wealth or name or station or any worldly endowment that might command others' respect. Jesus—who is

God himself—is born in a town where he and his family are utter strangers. They know no one who can house them, it seems, no rabbi willing to give them quarter in their desperation, and there is no room at the inn. Jesus' mother is thrown upon the backhanded mercy of an innkeeper apparently insensitive to her obvious need, in her last hours of pregnancy, for a place that is clean and comfortable. Jesus came to us, in other words, not as the powerful king the Israelites desired and expected, not as a mighty warrior or even a grown man who could do as he pleased, but as a newborn baby, the epitome of neediness.

I cannot get my mind around this, really. I remember my daughters at birth. Their eyes squinched shut. Needing to be fed and cleaned and diapered and kept warm. Incapable, as yet, of making their need known beyond whimpering or mouthing the air for the nipple. Needing to be carried everywhere. Incapable of standing or sitting, walking or even crawling toward some source of comfort or fulfillment. Not even as self-sufficient as a newborn calf or lizard.

When Jesus and his family return to their hometown of Nazareth, they are surely looked down on by neighbors and family. The baby was born too early to his supposedly devout parents, the neighbors discuss. A bastard. From birth, as Isaiah prophesies, Jesus was likely "despised and rejected" by others (Isaiah 53:3)—not only by those neighbors but probably by the pastor of his church as well.

And the child grows up. Had he grown up in the small town where I live, many would not have forgotten his illegitimacy, especially in the context of such a churchy family. Other children and their parents and even some of his teachers would have whispered mean things about him. He would have had to strive even harder than other kids to win favor in the locals' eyes. And maybe he wouldn't have. Such kids often don't strive to please. Some take up with even needier children—the poor, the unfashionable, the overweight, the smelly, the mentally retarded, outcasts all. Typically victims of others' cruelty have behavioral problems themselves. This one cringes all the time. That one never says anything or bullies weaker kids. By fifth grade or so, these needy ones are the kids I have to *command* my daughters to act kindly toward, and even then they may not. It is hard to like the unlikable, they tell me. Nay, impossible.

Those in education often regard the rejected and despised as the neediest of their pupils, yet they too struggle to like them. Such kids often cause trouble in class and aren't motivated to learn. Needy seventh- through ninth-graders are the worst, especially boys, teachers will tell you. They're so obnoxious. You can't teach them anything. They think they know everything.

Imagine Jesus in the temple at twelve, a seventh-grader, amazing all the experts with his knowledge and his answers to their questions and astonishing his parents with his behavior (Luke 2:47-48). The two words Luke uses in the passage, *astonished* and *amazed*, must be nearly synonymous in Greek, as the various English translations either interchange them or else substitute some other synonym, such as *astounded* or *bewildered* or *overwhelmed*, for one or the other. Although I share with Shakespeare, as Ben Jonson put it, "small Latine, and lesse Greeke,"[1] let me be bold and add *outraged* to the interpretive mix here in both instances. Martin Luther might concur. In his German translation of Luke 2:47-48, the teachers in the temple "*verwunderten sich*" (were amazed), whereas the parents "*entsetzten sich*" (were horrified).[2] In any case, surely those teachers were not only amazed but outraged at this kid's audacity, and his parents no less so.

By the time Jesus was grown up and preaching full time, he was perpetually outraging his listeners with his amazing, astonishing, astounding, bewildering, overwhelming claims and answers to questions. Shocking his listeners was a habit that didn't always win him friends and praise. Indeed, in another instance where Luke reports, using yet another Greek synonym, that Jesus "amazed" his audience—this time members of his own hometown synagogue—they end up driving him out of town and then taking him "to the brow of the hill on which the town was built, in order to throw him off the cliff" (Luke 4:29). The mob sounds pretty outraged to me.

Luckily, Jesus didn't need anyone to save him from the Nazarenes' murderous intentions. He just "walked right through the crowd and went on his way" (Luke 4:30). After all, Jesus is, as believers are taught, simultaneously man and God. He would point out a few years later when he was arrested for no reason that he could call on his Father at any moment to put "more than twelve legions of angels" at his disposal (Matthew 26:53). But he didn't save himself from torture or death, even though he could have. Right to the end he remained as despised and misrepresented and misunderstood—some might say pathetic—as he was in the beginning. And from that vantage point of what seems to be desperate need—the need to be loved and honored and recognized and truly revered as the King of kings and Lord of lords—he sits in judgment upon us still.

As a parent and as a teacher, I have often found myself in need on behalf of my charges. I need patience and longsuffering. I need resources for their benefit. I need compassion and mercy and profound understanding of their peculiar perspectives on things. I long for their enthusiasm, their remorse when they mess up and their appreciation of being forgiven, their kindness to one another. And for myself I desire, quite frankly, their love—love unadulterated by the fact that I am judging their progress or by their expectation that they will get something in return.

I believe, even if it is blasphemous, that God is like that. That, even though we are his creation and utterly powerless in comparison to him, he not only desires our love but needs it. Plain and simple. Like a newborn child, he needs us—to love him, to feed him, to protect him, to clap our hands in delight as he takes his first steps, to praise him when he sets those old guys in the temple on their heads.

Jesus says as much himself in his preview of the last judgment. "When the Son of Man comes in his glory, and all the angels with him," he declares, "he will sit on his glorious throne" and "separate the people one from another as a shepherd separates the sheep from the goats" (Matthew 25:31-32). And how will he judge them? On the basis of their attention to his needs: "I was hungry," he says he will tell us then; "I was thirsty. . . . I was a stranger. . . . I needed clothes. . . . I was sick. . . . I was in prison" (Matthew 25:35-36). He is referring—figuratively, of course—to the needs of those around us, but the resulting self-portrait of the deity is stunning. Even in his moment of greatest glory as the supreme power over all creation, Jesus characterizes himself as profoundly needy: hungry, thirsty, lonely, naked, sick, abandoned, and desperate for our love and nurture.

That's the Jesus I am worshiping this Christmas season: the one who not only loves us but so covets our love in return that he came as a whimpering, hungry, newborn baby—as needy and helpless as the very least among us.

8

ANOINTED

❧

If I, a woman, were to write a gospel of the entry of God into the world as one of us, I'm pretty sure I would not start with his human genealogy, as Matthew does. Or with Isaiah's prophecy about the coming of a messenger to "prepare the way for the Lord," as Mark does (Mark 1:3). Or with Luke's orderly account of that messenger's birth. And certainly not with John's spacy rendering of the Godman as the Word. No. I would start the account of God's birth the way any woman who has had a child would begin such a story—with the birth itself.

If I were Mary, say—who would certainly have had a unique and relevant experience of Jesus' life—I would begin my gospel with the gestation, perhaps providing details about my morning sickness and what I ate throughout my pregnancy and how much weight I gained. I would certainly mention that first astonishing movement of the Godfetus within me—so much like the bumping of a boat against an invisible mooring deep inside of me—and how the child the angel had spoken of became real to me at that moment.

But I would focus, as we women do, on the birth itself: on the contractions of my uterus to expel the child, on my pains, on the number of centimeters my cervix had dilated at each stage of the birth process, on the reports of the child's progress through the birth canal by whoever was in attendance and the eventual crowning of the baby's bluish scalp between my legs, on the blessed moment when the Godbaby left my body and, covered with my blood, took up a separate existence.

The actual birth of God in human form is a big event, full of irony and mystery and strange familiarity. It is bigger, to my mind, than every subsequent story of Jesus' life on earth, bigger even than the story of his death and resurrection, which could not have happened without the pain-wrought passage of the divine baby through an ordinary human cervix and vagina slick with birth fluids. The humblest of particulars for a Godbirth, if you ask me. Humbler even than the stable and grimy feed trough full of hay that served as Jesus' nursery and bassinet.

Actually, common though they are, births always seem to be important events. They figure frequently in films and TV shows because they are the quintessential story material: rich in

conflict and suspense, pain and waiting, fear, joy and sometimes sorrow. We always want to tell and hear tales of birth. At
the university where I work, I get regular e-mails announcing
births, noting not only the new baby's sex and name but also his
or her weight, length and disposition as well as the names of
proud parents, siblings and grandparents. I am not what I'd call
a "baby person"—someone who goes gaga over babies and begs
to hold every newborn she encounters—and I also habitually
delete all mass e-mails I receive. Nevertheless, when I see a
birth announcement in an e-mail's subject box, I always open
and read it.

Japanese writer Sei Shōnagon was the same way. A lady-in-
waiting for Empress Teishi, she left behind a detailed journal
called *The Pillow Book* describing her life in the tenth-century
Heian court.[1] Much of Sei Shōnagon's writing is in the form of
poetic lists: elegant things, things that should be large or small.
She mentions babies in numerous lists but apparently has little
love for them. She tolerates only babies who are pretty or plump
and resents any baby who cries when she is "trying to hear
something."[2] In a list extolling the loveliness of birds, she sourly
comments that "everything that cries in the night is wonderful.
With the exception, of course, of babies."[3] Yet she includes details of births—such as the expelling of the placenta or the arrival of a baby past its due date—in several lists of things one is
eager to learn. In "Things Whose Outcome You Long to
Know," she lists the gender of a newborn baby and goes out of
her way to specify that this is true even when the mother is

"some ordinary person or someone of low birth."[4] Something about birth stories seems to captivate even the least maternally inclined female audience.

Although I have never observed a human birth, I know the most intimate details of all my friends' children's births. Where and when the mother's water broke. How long she labored. Whether or not the baby immediately gave suck. And every detail, it seems to me, is another miracle. Miracle upon miracle, birth seems to me. My mother always said that a human birth she once attended was the greatest wonder she ever saw in her life. She couldn't even remember whose baby it was, only the birth itself.

When my husband and I ran cattle, the only task for which I would drop everything, entirely without rancor or regret, was assisting at the birth of a calf. Kris maintained that we had to stay out of the cow's way unless it was evident she wouldn't be able to have the calf without help—in other words, unless she had been at it without success for hours or had a string of pink goo dangling from her behind. If things were going badly, the calf might already be hanging limp from her haunches by the time we caught up with her and intervened. Or there might be a certain smell that meant she had been laboring fruitlessly throughout the night and the calf was now dead inside of her. Whatever the circumstances, we watched nervously from afar, using binoculars, and we approached cautiously so as not to disturb her concentration.

If it turned out we had to help, we first captured the cow, if possible, by luring her with feed to a pen or catching her head in a rope and tying her to a fence. As soon as we had her secured, we'd go to the barn for an arm-length plastic glove called a sleeve and the calf puller, an awkward metal contraption that just barely fit in the back of the pickup. Then we'd return, breathless, to the cow.

Kris always hoped, for the animals' sake, to find the deed accomplished, the cow chomping away at the slimy blob of placenta in the dirt while the calf thrashed into a standing position and butted its head at her udder to make her let down its first drink of milk—actually, the nutrient- and antibody-rich colostrum that would insure the calf's survival. But my own fascination with the birth process made me regret it when we missed out on the birth itself. The strange emergence of the calf's face and two slim feet beneath the cow's tail. The miraculous plopping of the newborn calf onto the dirt from a height of four feet or so without harm. The mother licking her baby in a first nudge toward health and independence. All of these moments in the birth of a calf were precious to me. I treasured them up in my heart and pondered them.

If, however, the birth was still not progressing when we got back with the calf puller, Kris would put on the sleeve and feel around inside the birth canal for the calf's feet. As soon as he found them and ascertained from their position the calf's orientation, he looped chains on the feet and tried pulling the calf out with his own strength. If that didn't work, he fastened the calf's feet to a cable on the calf puller while I held the wide part up against the cow's bottom, and then we'd winch the calf out. If all went well, the birth-wet calf would soon be lying on the ground before us.

Kris immediately set about freeing the cow, while I concerned myself with the calf. Usually it lay motionless with its eyes closed, and I was always terrified it was dead. I removed any membrane from its mouth and nose and tickled its nostril with a blade of grass to make it sneeze and, I hoped, breathe. I worked at the calf in dread until it finally opened its eyes and began struggling to stand and suck, and I was devastated if it never did. Most of the time, though, the calf survived. Afterward, regardless of the outcome, I always cried.

I had both of my daughters by Caesarean section. Grudgingly. Each after a full day of hopeful labor—twenty-seven long hours, in Charlotte's case. I was so exhausted by then that I no longer noticed my mother-in-law's overpowering perfume or my grad student friends chattering at my bedside or the mountain ridges of pain recorded on the fetal monitor. By the time the doctor decided the baby's heart would be in danger if it didn't come out soon, I was sleeping through massive contractions. They had to wake me up to insert the needle for the epidural between my vertebrae and prep me for surgery.

Soon I was lying spread-eagle on a table, the anesthesiologist fiddling with my wrists. Woozy from drugs and exhaustion, distracted by the surgeons' discussion of the astronauts on the TV screen floating on their tethers around space shuttle *Endeavor*, and separated from all view of the birth itself by a curtain, I was nonetheless alert to the moment at hand, the emergence of a slippery, wet being into the strange antiseptic metal world in which I lay, the holy metamorphosis of that first thud of life within me into a daughter. I wept. My husband, leaning helplessly over me, wept too.

The doctors and nurses didn't cry, I'm guessing. They were long since inured to this sort of miracle. They concentrated on the job before them, the sewing and cutting and washing and checking. Soon, I was in the cold recovery room, alone, dreaming hectic dreams, talking to a nurse, to Kris, to myself. Sooner still, the creature at the center of it all was sucking away at the magical food my body made. Eventually, I was crouching into our car, then straining backward to watch Kris fasten the buckle between the baby's little legs, and finally we were home.

I tell you all this to give you an idea of what all was left out of the story of the coming of the Messiah—or, literally, the Anointed One. Mary's labor. Joseph or perhaps some compassionate stranger attending. Their hours of hope and fear. Their exhaustion and relief when it was over. Someone's grubby knife cutting the umbilical cord. The whole embarrassing nature of birth itself, involving body parts not generally viewed or even mentioned in public, birth fluids deemed impure in most ancient cultures, and such potential humiliations as the accidental release of the mother's bladder or bowels. The messy, awkward realness of God's birth as a human being. The cursed result of Eve's sin, some might say. That's what God took on to save us from ourselves.

Of course, you might argue that God didn't see it that way. That, for him, birth—every revolting detail of it—is beautiful. When Jesus was born, God the Father was perhaps as wet-eyed as Kris and I were when witnessing our daughters' entries into the world. Or as my mother was at that forgotten woman's bed-side. As wet-eyed as I was even at the twitch of life in a calf we would soon sell. God likely watched over his own emergence from his human mother in unadulterated delight.

There is obscurity in this notion—the same obscurity that attends any examination of Jesus' dual existence as human and divine or even cursory consideration of the triune nature of God. How is it that Jesus, who was God himself, "grew in wis-dom and stature, and in favor with God" (Luke 2:52), as we're told he did? Later, on the cross, Jesus cries out, "My God, my God, why have you forsaken me?" (Mark 15:34). How could God forsake himself? And during Jesus' lifetime on earth, a Samaritan woman he meets at a well confidently exclaims, "I know that Messiah . . . is coming. When he comes, he will ex-plain everything to us" (John 4:25). If she is right—and Jesus himself confirms that she is when he responds, "I, the one speaking to you—I am he" (4:26)—she must be speaking of the complete revelations we'll all enjoy with Christ's second com-ing. Because Jesus did come, after all. He stood before her, drank water from her dipper, looked her directly in the eyes, spoke to her. Yet for now, so much remains unexplained.

Consider Jesus' entry into our world. Mary writhing and panting in the ill-lit stable. The carpenter Joseph, worried, inept, desperately reviewing in his mind a lamb's birth he had witnessed once in his long-ago youth. Those birth fluids. The blood-smeared infant mewing forth a faint protest from the scratchy hay in the feed trough.

This pathetic spectacle of a birth clothes all the mystery of the Almighty's promise to his otherwise doomed creatures. *I have come to save you from yourselves,* God tells us, *through one of your own—a Messiah, humbly anointed in amniotic fluid, in urine, in blood. I give you the very word of my own mouth, who is me. He was with me in the beginning. Through him all things—even you!—were made. Without him, nothing else exists. In him is life, and that life is the light of all people.*

9

TROUGHS

I've been thinking a lot about troughs this Christmas season. Around Thanksgiving, when the grass was dry and short, our neighbor Preston, who leases our pastures, dragged some troughs out into the field in front of our house to feed his cows. I barely noticed them. Preston and his cowboys are always driving in and out of our fields, moving big round hay bales in and out, setting out salt blocks, checking on their cattle or rounding them up for sale.

But then, a few days later at dawn, my husband pointed out some deer at the troughs, gleaning the feed pellets the cattle had scattered in the dirt. There were three deer: two big ones and a smaller one. Although they didn't seem to notice us looking at them or hear us whispering on our porch, they nevertheless ate in the watchful way of wild animals: raising their heads to listen with each bite, as if the feed had a sweet sound as well as a smell and a taste and they wanted to savor that too. So, for the past few weeks in the early morning, Kris and the girls and I have been watching the deer at Preston's feed troughs.

We've had an unusually dry summer and fall. The people around us who still raise cattle are all running out of water. Several of my husband's accounting clients sold their cows when their ponds dried up and it became too expensive to water them, and one afternoon Preston filled the big water trough—a straight-sided aluminum tub hooked up to a hydrant that holds about the amount of water in a Jacuzzi—down near the pens at my mother-in-law's house. Filling the water trough completely depleted my mother-in-law's well, which made her mad and embarrassed Preston, so we arranged to hook on to the rural water system. The project cost several thousand dollars—which Preston generously split with us—for membership in the Adair County Rural Water District as well as plumbing and ditch digging and two expensive freeze-proof tanks that we'll probably never need ourselves but that Kris says will raise our property value if we ever sell our farm. Which we probably won't. So, anyway, I've been thinking about those troughs.

And then, of course, there's the trough that Mary laid the newborn son of God in after having given birth in a stable. A trough mucky with manure like ours used to be, probably. According to biblical historians, the trough Jesus was laid in would have been made of stone or wood and probably projected from the wall of the stable.

His parents no doubt cushioned it with "a wad of hay," as Renaissance poet Edmund Spenser imagines in his poetic description of the birth in "An Hymne of Heavenly Love":

> Beginne from first, where he encradled was
> In simple cratch, wrapt in a wad of hay,
> Betweene the toylefull Oxe and humble Asse,
> And in what rags, and in how base aray,
>
> The glory of our heauenly riches lay,
>
> When him the silly Shepheards came to see,
> Whom greatest Princes sought on lowest knee.[1]

Spenser gets it exactly right, I think. The startling vulgarity of the scene. The simple cratch. (Think *crèche*.) The wad of hay. The rags. The silly Shepheards. Even Spenser's spelling startles in the twenty-first century.

I have recently been doing a spate of research about that cratch. At the risk of boring you with tedious etymological speculation that I find fascinating, here's what I have so far discovered. Spenser's word for *trough*, the Middle English word *cratch*—also spelled *cracche* and *cratche* back in the days when there were no spelling rules—is the same word John Wycliffe used in the nativity story in the first complete English translation of the Bible, published about two hundred years earlier: "And sche bare hir first borun sone, and wlappide hym in clothis, and leide hym in a cratche, for ther was no place to hym in no chaumbir" (Luke 2:7).[2]

The first "study Bible" in English, the 1599 annotated Geneva Bible of Calvin and his followers that became the Bible of New World Puritans, used *cratch* as well. The word derives from the Old High German *kripja*, the etymological ancestor of other onetime words for *trough*: *crib* and *cradle*. *Kripja* is also the root of the French word *crèche*, now used in English and French not only for the trough itself but for the entire setting of Jesus' birth: stable, trough and all. An even earlier translation than either Wycliffe's Bible or the Geneva Bible, the Anglo-Saxon Wessex Gospels of circa 990, called the trough by its Old English name, *binne*, as in feed bin today, a word that linguists think evolved from Celtic origins, along with an Italian word for dung cart. With the widespread popularization of the King James version of the Bible of 1611, though, most translations refer to the feed trough in which Jesus was laid as a manger, from the French *mangeoire*, a receptacle (the suffix *-oire*) out of which to eat (*manger*).

I hate the word *manger*. First off, it's French. I have nothing against the French in particular, and in fact, I love the language, to which I have committed eight or so years of coursework and a year of daily conversation. It's just that, although nothing could be more normal in language development than the influence of one language on another, it has always bothered me when one language supplants another. I hate that the Native American languages were all wiped out—some of them forcibly— by modern English, for example. And I can't abide the tone or attitude of those who argue for a one-language world or even a one-language country.

I think it would have been grand if the United States had ended up with more than one official language, as they almost did with German and English. Actually, my daughters tell me that we Americans have no official language, technically speaking, and have never had one. No language that, by law, must be used in the courts, government or other official venues. A bit of trivia they learned in school. In any case, while language variety may well be our punishment for the pride exhibited in the erection of the Tower of Babel—and God's confusing of language certainly does prevent us from communicating with one another without a significant investment of study and practice— still, as with all the rest of God's ideas, the end result is amazingly good, in my opinion. I love languages.

So, it has always especially bothered me that the Anglo-Saxons surrendered not only their country but their very language when they were conquered by the French in 1066. But then, the Anglo-Saxons themselves, when they took over a few centuries before that, had eradicated the language of England's original Celts. And then there's the Latin of the Roman conquerors and of the clergy they left behind to win the people of England to Christ, which effected the same sort of erasure of the common tongue, at least among those writing books. The Romans were so nearly successful that King Alfred initiated the first literacy campaign—in the ninth century!—to preserve and promote the language of ordinary people. In hundreds of countries all over the world to this day, linguists and Bible translators are attempting language recoveries by similar methods, and I applaud their efforts.

There's a bigger problem with the word *manger*, though, than its hegemonic origins, and it is this: We don't use *manger* for anything other than what Jesus was laid in when he was born. My husband says farmers do: that when he dairied he used the word to refer to a special trough attached to a wall—a sort of bin or rack in which to put feed or hay for the cows to chomp on while the milkers are being attached.

But no one else I know of would use the word *manger* today to mean trough. A manger, for most, is a comfy little bassinet lined with a silky-looking substance many have never actually touched and thus don't realize is rough and scratchy enough to abrade a newborn's tender skin. And, for most of those who use the word *manger*, there is only one such bassinet in all of history, the one in which Mary laid the Christ child. The word *manger* is a cheat. In it, the most electrifying message of the gospel—that God lowered himself to become one of us as his way of saving us—lies buried beneath numbing wads of linguistic development, minimally recorded history and gnarled church tradition.

God's baby lay in a feed trough, not in a manger. A crude depression hacked into a ledge in a dingy stall, an unsophisticated receptacle that large animals drooled in and shat on and that rats visited nightly, leaving their droppings. The son of God so emptied himself out of his deity and power and sheer dignity that he allowed himself to be not only squeezed out of a gooey orifice in a homely human body in the dark corner of a stable but wrapped in rags and, yes, probably that wad of hay Spenser envisioned and then laid—for safety's sake, to keep from being rolled over on—in the least hygienic of neonatal cradles: a dirty feed trough few people these days would want to touch. All of these details of God's plan are lost in the cozy word *manger*.

My students, I recently discovered, don't even know what a feed trough is, much less a manger. They were reading aloud their translations of a story—one of my favorites—that the Brothers Grimm collected from their Hessian neighbors back in the nineteenth century. We call the Grimm brothers' stories "fairy tales," but, as J. R. R. Tolkien wisely pointed out, if a story has no fairies or other supernatural elements, it's not properly a fairy tale at all.[3] The Grimm brothers themselves called the folktales they collected *Kinder- und Hausmärchen*, literally "children- and house-tales," and I think that's a good name for most of them, especially the one I had asked my students to translate. It relates an ordinary episode from a typical household of the Grimms' time: a couple and their young son and the elderly grandpa eating dinner, an episode that could occur in a typical household today, in families like our own if people were still in the habit, as they were in the Grimms' time, of living with their elderly parents.

The story is called "The Old Grandfather and the Grandson."[4] It's short, and if you don't know it, you should, so I'll tell it here in my own translation:

Once upon a time there was a stone-old man—so old that his eyes had become dim and his ears deaf and his knees shaky. At dinnertime, he could barely hold the spoon, and soup splattered all over the tablecloth and dribbled from his mouth. His son and daughter-in-law were disgusted and made the old man sit in the corner, behind the stove, where they wouldn't have to see him eat. They gave him his food in a cheap clay bowl—and hardly enough to satisfy him at that—and he sat by himself at mealtime, glancing toward the table with sad, wet eyes. Sometimes his hands shook so much that he couldn't even hold his bowl, and once it fell to the floor and broke. The young wife yelled at him, but he only sighed. So she went out and bought him a wooden bowl for a few cents, and he had to eat out of that.

There they sat, one day, at dinner, while the little grandson played with blocks on the floor.

"What are you building there, Son?" his father asked him.

"I'm building a little trough for you and Mama to eat out of, when I get big," he told them.

The man and his wife looked at each other a long while, and then both of them started to cry. They fetched the old man to the table and from then on always let him eat with them and said nothing when he made a little mess.

My students' translations were all different and interesting and very good, except for this business of the "little trough." The word is *Tröglein* in German, the child's diminutive version of the noun *Trog*, for which my students' German-English dictionaries gave a variety of options not at all relevant to the circumstances. Using these entries and their thesauruses, my students translated the word variously as a *chest*, *trunk*, *tray* or *depression*. A couple of them—in an admirable attempt to make sense of the story, which I had told them was the most important goal of translation—opted to contradict the diminutive suffix "-*lein*" in *Tröglein* and came up with "a big bowl." With the mistranslation of a single word, their translations missed the point of the story altogether.

"Why would he make them eat out of a chest or a tray?" I prodded them. "What's the sense in that? Or even a big bowl? What kind of big bowl would we be talking about here? Is it bigger than the wooden bowl the daughter-in-law bought to replace the clay one? And for that matter, why does she buy the old grandfather a wooden bowl the second time around?"

We talked that through until they finally guessed that, in the days of the Grimms, wood was cheaper than even clay and, more importantly, it was less breakable. Translated into contemporary crockery options, we figured out together, the peevish wife would have bought her father-in-law a cheap plastic bowl from the Dollar Store, a bowl one might use for a child.

But that still left the little boy on the floor with his blocks.

"What was he building?" I asked my students. I gave them the hint that the etymology of the word *Trog* was the Old High German word for *tree*, which, since Old High German and Old English were just about the same language, had the same etymology as the English word they needed.

"A big wooden bowl," a student offered, tracing the curve of her nose-ring thoughtfully with the edge of one long fingernail. But that wasn't it entirely.

"What's the old man's problem?" I persisted. "Why do they make him sit in the corner in the first place?"

"He spills his soup all over the place," she said.

"Yes, but why?"

"He can't hold a spoon. Because he shakes too much."

"Well, so, then, when the little boy's parents get old and shaky, how will what their son is building solve that problem? Won't they still have to use spoons with a big wooden bowl?"

"He's just a kid. He probably didn't think of that," one of my lazier students rationalized. These were first-year students, fresh out of high school. Translation, they had been discovering all semester, was hard work, and a number of them resisted on principle.

"I know, I know!" another student called out from the back of the room. "It's a big bowl that they can eat out of without spoons. You know, like animals. They could just lap up their soup like animals."

"Yes!" I told them. "Like what an animal eats out of. And what would that be called?"

Silence. Eventually someone offered, "A dog dish."

"My dogs eat out of an old oil pan," another student said.

"We just use a big bowl."

And so we were back to the big bowl, and I eventually had to just tell them that this was one of the rare cases in translation where just one word would work. A trough.

"In German, as in English," I told them, "*trough* is an old-fashioned word, although it still is used today in such technical expressions as 'low-pressure trough' and the trough part of a rain gutter. And if you're a farmer, of course, you use the word all the time. And in the Grimms' time, everyone was a farmer."

Feed troughs in the early nineteenth century, I told them, would likely have been wooden, like the grandfather's unbreakable bowl. A few crude boards nailed together. Possibly something as rudimentary as a hollowed-out log. Cheaply made but sturdy enough to hold up if the livestock kicked it or climbed up in it, as our cows used to like to do. The key traits you're looking for in a trough, I explained, are size—so that all the livestock can get their heads in at the same time—and durability.

A couple of them nodded wisely, and I was encouraged, even though I know from experience that certain students tend to nod wisely precisely when they have no idea what you're talking about or why you're going on about it.

I asked them to picture the feed troughs they had seen. It turned out that, although we live in a cattle-ranching part of the Ozarks and several of the students were locals, not one of them could tell me what contemporary feed troughs were like. So, since one of my goals in teaching them how to translate in the first place was to make them aware of the vast gulf between different languages and the cultures behind them, I decided to instruct them about the difference between the lives of the small farmers they lived among and their own. This was what we call, in my profession, a teachable moment. And anyway, I hate passing up an opportunity to educate people who eat meat and drink milk and may one day be invited to vote on this or that farm-related issue.

Nowadays, I told them, feed troughs for cattle are typically made of thick plastic boards in a heavy metal frame about ten feet long. They cost about a hundred dollars each, which is about how much a newborn calf costs if you buy one to raise it up with a bottle, as my daughters used to do most springs. That's a fair investment, I pointed out, when you consider that, back when my husband and I farmed, we raised only about a hundred calves a year and had to buy many such implements just to keep things going. Feed troughs. Water troughs. Bale rings. Mineral feeders. Not to mention even more costly mechanical tools like tractors and hay equipment.

Some farmers, to save money, make their own feed troughs out of discarded water heater tanks. To make one, you use a torch to cut in half a water heater tank—which I had to explain was not the flimsy white metal exterior housing you see in the cupboard but an interior iron vessel that none of them even knew was inside. Then you weld a length of rebar bent into a V onto each end to make four legs. One discarded tank, which people ordinarily have to pay to get rid of, makes two fair feeders four or five feet long for the price of the welding and a great saving of landfill space. That's what we call recycling out in the country, I said.

Water-heater troughs are somewhat rickety and hard to move, though. So, if you're feeding a herd of any size or don't have heavy-duty welding equipment, you will probably buy the plastic ones, which have runners along the bottom so that you can drag them from field to field with a tractor or shove them up into a pickup bed and slide them around by hand in the field. Portability is another trait you are likely to want in a trough, I summarized. (Once I'm off on one of my topics, there's no stopping me.) You want to be able to move a trough easily from one field to another and in and out of working pens. That way you can use feed to get the cattle to go where you want them to go.

Kris and I were of the "lure" rather than the "drive" persuasion of farmers. We never chased our cows or yelled and hooted at them, as Preston's cowboys did. Instead, we catered to the cows' psychological traits to manage them. Cattle, for example, are ritualistic in the extreme. They follow a daily grazing routine so rigidly determined that they wear paths into the grass between their daily stops. Their favorite shade tree. The pond. The mineral feeder. The nursery for their calves: an unofficial gathering place for recently born bulls and heifers, typically presided over by a few of the younger cows. If you observe the cows' movements and take them into account, you can use your resulting knowledge of where they'll be at a given time to manage them more efficiently.

Cattle get skittish and wily if you try to get them to go into a new field, I said, even if it's close by and the forage there is better and they've been reaching their heads through the barbed-wire fence for weeks to get at the taller grass. So if we wanted to move cattle into a new pasture, we first fed them for a few days in troughs we set up near the gate. Then, as soon as they got used to seeing us coming with the feed buckets, we just led them on through the gate and into the new field.

To feed, you set several troughs up in a row and pour feed from buckets down the length, preferably all in one go so as to avoid being trampled and possibly killed when the cattle charge from all directions toward the rattle of the feed on the plastic and the sweet smell of corn and molasses. After a minute or two of frenzied shuffling, the cattle line up alongside the troughs and lick up feed with their gigantic tongues and munch away. As they finish in one spot at the trough, they back up and push in at another, looking for a place with more feed. Friskier heifers will jump up into the trough itself in their excitement, or nose the trough up against the cows on the other side. As they eat, they squirt out happy jets of blackish-green manure, splattering one another, sometimes right in the face.

So the troughs get dirty over time. And rusted. And bent. In a year or two, a trough's runners will have rusted through or its plastic liner will have popped out of the frame or, if it's a water-heater trough, one of its legs will have twisted out of shape or broken off entirely. To save money, you'll probably keep on using it. A farmer with welding equipment might try welding a new leg on, but soon it will break again. And there's nothing you can do to fix a rusted runner on a store-bought trough. In time it is nothing more than a curved pane of plastic propped against a twisted frame, and you have to invest in a new one, or five or six new ones, along with a new mineral feeder and a slew of bale rings, which have also rusted apart. And so you see why so many farmers have gone bust in recent years.

Of course, these are just the troughs of my experience, and we had only a small farm, at our height only one hundred thirty or so head of mama cows. The wealthier ranches we visited when we were shopping for bulls sometimes had more expensive concrete troughs that were surely more durable, but not at all portable. Bulls, unless they are running with the herd, are usually penned and grain-fed, so being able to move their troughs around isn't as important.

We ran out of class time before I was able to make any kind of connection between the Grimm brothers' trough and the troughs on farms of today, much less that Christmas trough I had been thinking about. This happens to me a lot, as you can probably guess. Occasionally students condemn my discursive habits on teacher evaluations. "She often chases after rabbits," a student once wrote. I suppose he or she was right.

But if I were ever asked to give an evaluation of my students other than the grades I give them on their coursework, I would probably fault most of them for being mechanical in their learning habits. Students are like cattle, I find. They love the rituals of syllabi and study guides and PowerPoint outlines telling them everything they are expected to know. "Is this going to be on the test?" they ask, and the underlying message—to me, to everyone else in class—is, "If this isn't going to be on the test, what's the value in learning it?" You have to wheedle and scheme and feed them sweet feed to take them beyond their habitual classroom expectations, beyond words and ideas they're sure they already know to the real meanings hidden, like newborn bunnies in wads of hay their mothers have secreted in their tangled warrens beneath the pasture.

In the beginning of the book of Isaiah, the Lord laments, in the words of Wycliffe, "An oxe knew his lord, and an asse knew the cratche of his lord; but Israel knewe not me, and my puple vndurstood not."[5] In the words of Calvin's Geneva Bible, written two centuries later, it's "The oxe knoweth his owner, and the asse his masters crib: but Israel hath not knowen: my people hath not vnderstand."[6] And in the King James Version, written a dozen years after that, "The ox knoweth his owner, and the ass his master's crib: but Israel doth not know, my people doth not consider."

Even now, after my half-hour speech on troughs, I don't know if my students would really understand what these words mean, even in their preferred version of Scripture, the NIV, a translation written during their lifetimes at the seventh-grade reading level:

The ox knows its master,
    the donkey its owner's manger,
but Israel does not know,
    my people do not understand. (Isaiah 1:3)

They would see the word *manger* and miss it all.

Consider, I would tell them in that teachable moment. This is the Lord God speaking, our Creator, whose first interaction with the humans he had created was to feed them, offering them "all kinds of trees . . . that were pleasing to the eye and good for food" (Genesis 2:9). Here is, in other words, our Master, our Owner, our Father, longing wistfully for even such notice of his provision as animals devote to their feed troughs. *The loyal ox recognizes its master,* the God who made us is saying. *Even the stubborn donkey, though it is likelier to follow its own will than mine, at least knows where its feed trough is. But Israel neither recognizes its Master nor knows where to go to be fed. My own people persist in not seeing me. Blind and hungry and lost, they bumble stupidly away from the hand that wants nothing but to feed and caress them, that longs for nothing but to lead them home.*

And it was out of this yearning to be recognized by his most beloved creatures, this longing to provide for them and lead them back to himself, that God stooped from beyond the starry sky to the doorway of that stable long ago and lowered his tiny, perfect, newborn Self, wrapped in rags, into a grimy feed trough wadded with hay.

IO

WASHING SOCKS

Many years ago I taught English for a year at a university in China. It was a strange period in my life, pleasantly lonely and slow, with few contours: nothing major accomplished, no enduring relationships established, an interlude virtually eventless that left few enduring marks on my psyche.

I lived alone in a two-room, all-concrete apartment in a building that housed a dozen or so other "foreign experts," as we were called. I got up in the morning, made my solitary breakfast, taught my morning classes and returned to my apartment for the two-hour lunchtime siesta to find that the *ayis*— or "aunties," the Chinese name for female household workers—had been there in my absence to make up my bed and mop the floors. During my siesta, I read or dozed out on my concrete balcony. Then I taught my afternoon class and returned to the apartment.

Looking back, I see that year as a magical period of my life, although I didn't know it then. When nothing at all mattered and the slightest detail made all the difference in the world. At the time, though, I felt mainly bored and idle and vaguely irritated with myself for being so, waiting for something to happen, certain nothing would happen. I was conscious of the passage of minutes.

Many of the other foreign experts, I discovered not long after my arrival, were missionaries in hiding who had applied for teaching positions as a way to enter the country and spread their particular gospel. There was a Roman Catholic priest from France, a Mormon couple and a youngish woman—a little older than I was—who called herself "just Christian" and had spent several years in Pakistan before her time in China.

The presence of vocal believers made me aware of my own absence of faith in ways I didn't expect. I observed them closely and questioned them, looking for damning contradictions or incontrovertible evidence of wisdom, trying to figure them out. The priest held secret Masses all by himself at four o'clock every morning, I learned as I got to know him. The Mormons wouldn't drink the Chinese tea served everywhere—because of the caffeine content, they said when I asked—and drank instead expensive imported soft drinks that I guessed had just as much caffeine. And although the Christian woman held noisy worship services in her apartment once a week, she seemed somehow even lonelier than I was. She never attended any of the frequent banquets in honor of visiting dignitaries to which the foreign experts were always invited, and everyone was always forgetting her name. In short, I found my missionary colleagues' habits of faith equally alien—and alienating—and full of the absurdities I expected.

Nevertheless, their shared certainty, however illogical, somehow intensified my loneliness and sparked in me a faint longing. I wished I believed in something as intensely as they did. But what faith I'd had as a child—a blithe consciousness of God's presence that was nothing like what these people appeared to believe—had left me years before.

The Catholic priest should have made the most sense to me, since I grew up Catholic myself, but in many ways he was the most foreign. Jean-Pierre had lived in China for years and spoke good Chinese, but no English. Since I didn't then know Chinese, language was a barrier between us until I got past the embarrassment of using the schoolbook French of my high school and college years. Language was just a small part of what separated us, though. Jean-Pierre came from an old school of Catholicism totally unlike the laissez faire faith of my youth and had a set of emphatic-sounding convictions that reminded me of a book of martyrs I liked to read as a child and the stories my dad told of his Irish Catholic upbringing. Nuns. Purgatory. Lent. Dire vows made in childhood. Jean-Pierre had decided on the priesthood at age six, during his mother's funeral.

There was a Chinese Catholic church in Beijing—practicing pretty much the same thing as ordinary Catholicism, someone told me, except without the pope—and I wanted Jean-Pierre to attend Mass there with me and see what it was like. He was mysteriously against it. I speculated that he'd had some bad experience with Chinese Catholics—something that, out of his habitual reluctance to be critical of others, he wouldn't tell me. I pried until he finally explained that he had long known about the local Catholics but refused to have anything to do with them out of loyalty to the pope. The explanation confused me even more. As a child believer, I had never paid much attention to the pope. The Vatican, the cardinals in their red robes and skullcaps, encyclical pronouncements issued in English that sounded like Latin—all that seemed so far away, both in time and in place, so distant from my childish experience of God as the repository of my small prayers and hopes.

Sometime in my growing-up years I was taught that the pope's words only obtained their famous infallibility when he spoke ex cathedra—from his throne—which he had only ever done a few times in the history of the church. Even then, he only spoke out on esoteric matters of doctrine that I never gave much thought to, such as that Mary—like Jesus after his resurrection—had been assumed directly into heaven instead of having to endure the indignity of the grave like the rest of us. If the pope only had to be right about stuff like that, I had decided as a teenager, I was happy to grant him authority in the church, and I never thought much about it.

When I tried to explain all this to Jean-Pierre and question him about how the pope was viewed in the church he grew up in, we soon reached one of our frequent cultural impasses. Our conversations had by then a reliable if frustrating structure—rather like a discussion with someone very hard of hearing—that I had come to cherish. Faced with what I was sure was my own misunderstanding of something he'd said in a conversation about the Holy Spirit, say, or how to make a *pâte brisée*, I would snatch and blather my way through an incredulous question. Jean-Pierre repeated what I had been trying to say as a statement, in solid French that made sense to both of us, and nodded his head in hearty confirmation. Even then, I was always convinced that he was merely affirming that this was what I had meant and not what he really thought. So I repeated my question, using his more correct phrasing but subtly jerking and intoning the words in hopes of getting at what I still didn't understand and offering him an opportunity to refine or disclaim some part of it—which, of course, he never did. This little liturgy of misunderstanding would continue until we eventually gave up on the topic and started a new game of *crapette*, an evil French version of double solitaire to which he was addicted.

Somehow I managed to drag Jean-Pierre with me to the Beijing cathedral anyway. Just to see, I coaxed. I figured I wouldn't understand anything unless a Chinese speaker attended with me. There we found a pre–Second Vatican Council congregation of believers, intoning in Latin the Mass my father had grown up with, the Mass Jean-Pierre had grown up with, too, for he was considerably older than I was. Jean-Pierre cried into his shoulder. I was perplexed and somewhat amused, but largely unmoved.

The Mormon couple had a newborn and were caught up, pretty much, in taking care of him. They had arrived in China thoroughly prepared for what they would find there. The husband had taught himself passable Chinese before their arrival, and they had brought their own Mormon textbooks from which to teach history and grammar. When I questioned them on matters of faith, they were surprisingly unforthcoming. They had a Bible prominently displayed in their apartment, though, and they told me they were Christians.

So, when I found the students in my Survey of English Literature course ignorant on the subject of the faith that informed almost every work of literature we read, I invited the Mormon woman to my class to explain it to them. She told the parable of the lost sheep to demonstrate what she said was the central idea of Christianity: the importance of each individual person to God. The story shocked my students—who were aghast at the shepherd for abandoning all the other sheep to go after just one—and puzzled me. Individualism was a concept I had never considered in the context of Christianity. The Mormons' faith, I decided, was more political than religious, and it was political in a way that, as the aspiring communist I was in those days, I found especially noxious to the public good: all about a person's rights and quite mum on topics I revered, such as sharing resources equally and collective responsibility for social ills.

The "just Christian" woman who lived in the apartment next to mine baffled me the most, though. We generally talked on our shared landing as we fiddled for our keys coming and going. She told me the story of how, back on the farm in Nebraska, she had received an anonymous donation by mail in the exact amount she had been praying for to take her on her first mission trip abroad. The same thing happened when, a little later, she had no money and wanted to go to Pakistan to tell the lost about God, and again when she wanted to go to China. God, it seemed, was always sending her money. Although she had lived in China for several years, she knew no Chinese at all beyond the sentence she taught me the first day I met her: *Wo bu ming bai*, which means "I don't understand." It was a sentence she used so often, she said, that she was sure I would need it too. Spelled phonetically in my mind the way she said it, the phrase effectively summed up my initial experience of everything I encountered in China: "Whoa! Booming by!"

I suspected my neighbor may have felt that way about her experiences abroad as well, as she invested mightily in maintaining an entirely American life wherever she went. She got all her food either at the Friendship Store, where only foreigners could shop, or from boxes sent by her family back in the States. When I went to her apartment, I found items in her refrigerator that, in my years abroad, I had forgotten even existed. American cheese. Puffy white bread. Ketchup. A Tupperware container of sweet, mustardy coleslaw.

The other Americans who snuck up the stairwell to worship

with her once a week seemed just like her. They brought plastic tubs of macaroni salad and pimiento-flecked cheese spread to share after the last rollicking hymn, and together they celebrated a God I had never even heard of: one who put money in an envelope and licked a stamp and sent it off, via U.S. mail, to a zealous teenage girl on a corn farm in Nebraska.

Although I was intrigued by my neighbors' religiosity and secret doings—Jean-Pierre's middle-of-the-night acts of charity on behalf of the *ayis*, the long underwear I discovered the Mormon woman wore even in the hottest weather, the rowdy singing I heard through my cinder-block walls—I nevertheless felt most at home among the foreign experts who were *not* missionaries and who got together regularly to drink Beijing beer and argue and joke. I often pooled my groceries with one or the other household, and we shared a stir-fry of whatever we had. Sometimes we went out to a local dumpling joint or to the fancy Beijing Hotel for their famous Dan Dan noodles. One of the women, a longtime resident of China, included me in her regular trips to the beauty salon for a hair wash and head massage, and her elderly Dutch husband accompanied me to the Chinese opera, his passion, and whispered English translations of the Chinese characters projected on the wall beside the stage.

One cold afternoon, the unmarried Australian couple from the first floor invited me to a party at one of the former summer palaces, an abandoned landmark of Beijing's imperial past that, like most others, had fallen into disrepair during the Cultural Revolution. The half-decayed buildings of the palace, with their brightly painted eaves, sprawled around a storybook lake nestled in a forest of black-limbed trees. There, a compatriot of theirs—a young businessman negotiating one of the joint ventures then becoming popular—lived in the enviable, otherworldly solitude that moneyed foreigners, like Washington Irving living in the Alhambra, had enjoyed in another century. The man's company had rented for him all the palace's habitable space—several large rooms furnished with layered rugs and heavy antique furniture—and he lived there like a banished prince, waited and doted upon by Chinese servants.

It was early winter, coming up on Christmas, and the lake was frozen solid. We all put on skates—many of the guests had brought their own and an *ayi* brought out a box of all sizes for those of us who hadn't—and sailed around the lake until it got too cold to stand up. Then we had dinner at a nearby restaurant and returned to the red-carpeted rooms to drink toddies and sing Christmas carols late into the night.

I need to say here that, although I do not have an especially good voice or much knowledge of music, there are few things I like better than getting together with other people—especially strangers, with new songs and enthusiasms—to sing. As a child I took magical car trips—to beaches and skiing and rock collecting—with my best friend, whose mom taught us the exotic songs of her British childhood: Elizabethan rounds in which church bells had names like Great Tom and harts and hinds and little pretty roes leapt about the greenwood and girls were charged to "serve well the black sow all on a misty morning."[1]

Some of my fondest memories of my years abroad include singing "Oh! Susanna"[2]—the American anthem, in the Chinese perspective of that time—at virtually every banquet I attended in China and Elvis Presley songs all night long with a group of elderly yodelers in the Swiss Alps. I like learning others' songs and teaching them mine, and I especially love that blissful moment when our disparate sounds all merge into one and my pitiful little voice becomes part of something larger and better. I don't care who my fellow singers are or what kind of music we sing. Even the silliest song will work.

Here is a vision of heaven I find far more compelling these days than the staid hymn-singing I envision when I read Revelation: I am sitting at a table with Jesus and his friends and some of mine and maybe even a few of our former enemies, and we're drinking wine and eating bread with pepper and crunchy salt and good green olive oil, and between bites we're singing, "Well rung, Tom Boy! Well rung, Tom! Ding dong, cuckoo! Well rung, Tom!"[3]

That evening in those snug rooms at that idyllic palace, I was, in other words, in an entirely secular, winter-wonderland version of what would one day be my vision of heaven: eating, drinking, singing. Surrounded by red carpets and luxury and smiling *ayis* offering me dainties on plates. It was a lot like my teenage dream of Christmas, the one you see pictures of in magazines and hear about in songs, with logs crackling in the fireplace and rosy-faced women wearing evening dresses of paisley and black velvet, and laughing men tipping bottles of wine, and everyone lifting glasses and voices, singing and happy.

Australians, as it turned out, sing different carols than we Americans, and one they all loved was a song I had never heard before about the shepherds being visited by angels on the night of the nativity. Everyone there knew enough of it that they were able to reconstruct, between them, several verses. Once they all agreed on the words, they boomed them out, no doubt filling the cold blackness beyond those warm rooms with their voices. The first verse went like this:

> While shepherds watched their flocks by night
> all seated on the ground,
> an angel of the Lord came down,
> and glory shone around.

> Fear not, said he, for mortal dread
> had filled their troubled mind,
> Glad tidings of great joy I bring
> for thee and all mankind.[4]

I found it irritating—but also amusing—that the shepherds in the song all shared one "troubled mind." It was the sort of mistake I was always correcting on students' papers, clearly necessitated by the rhyme with "mankind." The Australians, who had been singing the song from childhood, had never particularly noticed it, they said. As the evening progressed, we sang the song more than once, and eventually someone started in on the Jingle-Bells-Batman-Smells version they all knew from childhood: "While shepherds washed their socks by night all seated on the ground, an angel of the Lord came down and glory shone around." Nowadays, the silly image of shepherds washing their socks comes back to me every Advent, whenever I read their part of the Christmas story. In fact, in the years following that night—initially unhappy years during which I moved from country to country before I returned for good to the country of my birth and finally came to believe in the angel's glad tidings of great joy—that vision of the shepherds' story has become my primary picture of Christmas night.

It was an ordinary work night for the shepherds, in my imagination. There were five or six of them. They had followed their usual rotation to end up out in the country somewhere west of Bethlehem and had found a good place for the sheep to bed down. It was cool out and very clear. Not snowing or anything, but nippy enough for them to lean in toward the fire, which they had been letting die down after a shared meal of curds, bread and lentil soup. They passed around the last dregs from one shepherd's wineskin that he said he may as well share as drink all alone.

The pasture had not been good that year, and they were all feeling glum. They were independent operators, but just barely, having hired out for years before they were able to put together small flocks of their own. One of their number had recently been bought out by a guy they had all known from childhood, a used-to-be friend who now had nothing to do with them and owned several flocks of his own. He and his hired men had an uncanny ability to arrive at the good grass before they did. Not only that, but prices for lambs had been dropping. One of the shepherds was thinking about selling his flock and getting out of the sheep business altogether, but he didn't know what else he could do for a living. Another of the shepherds had newborn twin daughters back at home—two little shiny-eyed lambs, he called them—but he was worried about his wife's lethargy and milk supply and whether he'd be able to support two more children.

The shepherds had worked out a schedule of who was on watch when, but it wasn't quite time for sleep, so they filled their cookpot with water and set it over the fire so they could wash their underclothes and socks. As they scrubbed, they reverted to a conversation they'd had earlier in the day—about the promises of their God toward those who tried, as they did, to follow his rules for righteous behavior. Promises of long, prosperous lives. The humble would be lifted up, they discussed. The hungry fed. The righteous vindicated. A messiah, one of their own, would lead them into true contentment.

It was hard to believe these promises, they all agreed, but they were trying. Failing mostly, one of them said. And into this ordinary event, this washing of socks and worrying about the future and reflecting upon—and questioning and doubting, even—the gleaming promises of a loving God, came the booming voice of an angel, roaring, "Do not be afraid!" and proclaiming the fulfillment of their most precious hopes: "I bring you good news that will cause great joy for all the people.

Today in the town of David a Savior has been born to you; he is the Messiah, the Lord" (Luke 2:10-11).

Today. Right in our hometown. Born to us, they thought. And possibly they were even then discounting—as people tend to do in the presence of miracles—what they had just heard with their own ears and seen with their own eyes as a hallucination, inspired by their sleepy conversation and the wine they had been drinking. But then, in that moment of doubt, more angels appeared, lots of them, filling the sky with their glory and singing. And what the shepherds had hoped for against all reason and perhaps still yet doubted—what a couple of them had rejected altogether, in this or that crisis of daily living—was all at once realized.

Today.

Here.

For us.

And they wrung out their socks and made their way to the stable in the town of David, where the angel had said they would find the child wrapped in rags, lying in a feed trough.

What can that have been like?

I was, as I have said, an atheist when I heard the song of the shepherds washing their socks. The faith of my childhood was—in those eventless and meaningless days in China—a distant thing, of almost forgotten value, a comforting collection of promises remembered mainly as absences. The absence of an ear that heard the silent prayers I had long since given up saying. The lack of any certainty about what was true or what mattered. The sadness and abandonment I always felt at Christmastime, when weird, barely intelligible hopes welled up inside me.

A younger Christian friend of mine once told me she had trouble understanding the Jews' longing for the Messiah. Although I too have had trouble with the notion of a messiah—especially given what seems to me the dearth of explicit scriptural statements saying that God had promised one in the first place—I've never had any trouble identifying with the Jews' longing for a savior. Everything in me yearns—has always yearned—in the days leading up to Christmas, although as a nonbeliever I was never sure for what.

As a child, I had longed, of course, for material things. That Easy-Bake Oven that my parents never got me because, as they said, I could use the real oven any time I wanted. And that red-haired doll in the Sears Catalog that spoke Spanish.

There was something else, though. Something that winter snow and the grit and smell of dead leaves trodden underfoot and those merry pictures in magazines somehow reminded me of—a yearning less definable or attainable, a hope bigger and cheerier and more important. Like everyone, I longed for love: to love someone and be loved back. And for connectedness in general. For certainty. For the confidence that life was more than what I saw around me or even the sure knowledge, however resigned, that this world was all there was, that I knew what there was to know about existence and this was all there would ever be.

But it was none of these benefits that I yearned for at Christmastime, exactly. No, I think it was genuine jollity, just that: glad tidings, great joy, piercing the everyday and changing everything. A moment, like the shepherds' moment, coming in the midst of the usual worries and catastrophes and firsthand knowledge that all is *not* well in the world, a vision cutting through the ordinary doubts and smug rejections, a moment when the opportunity to believe the old promises intrudes itself into our daily experience. When our sock-washing is suddenly illuminated by glory and songs and we experience the ecstatic fulfillment of whole generations of hoping. The moment when we realize—we must!—that now, today, right here, to us, a child is born, and nothing will ever be the same again.

II

IN THE BLEAK
MIDWINTER

I have read that holiday depression is a myth, that suicides don't really go up, as people often say they do, during what should be the happiest season of the year, when we celebrate the birth of God in our world. I find this hard to believe, even though I know that my own bouts of Christmastime despair—a legacy of my encounter with crime—are merely an accident of bad timing. For me, the holiday season marks not only the reassuring anniversary of Jesus' advent into our world but also, alas, the wretched anniversary of my first real encounter with the sort of violence and terror that has typified our world since the days of

Cain and that has traumatized me yearly ever since.

Coincidentally, the assault happened at the end of fall semester, in the last days before the Christmas break. I was in
graduate school then. In my early twenties. Rather late in life to
have my first real encounter with evil, as I viewed the experience in the years that followed. Before that night I had never
really believed in evil.

Certainly not in my own evilness. I'd erred like everyone
else, of course—sometimes seriously enough to regret the consequences for a long time. Nevertheless, in the handful of times
in my Catholic youth when I had officially confessed my sins—
regular confession was going out of fashion in those days—I'd
had to think hard to come up with a satisfactorily grim-sound-
ing list of sibling fights and disobediences to my parents, and I
totted them off to the bored priest behind the screen entirely
without remorse.

Sins, in my child mind, were mistakes. Regrettable only if
they got you in trouble. Inevitable and unintended, like stains,
as the nun in my catechism class taught us to think of them.
Stains, my mother was also teaching me in those days, were not
likely to be permanent as long as you used the right combination, in the right order, of hot or cold water and detergents, de-
pending on the type of stain you were dealing with. Repen-
tance was not a spiritual matter so much as a method of stain
removal. And the stains themselves were not the product of *evil*,
as I understood the word. Evil, if there was such a thing at all,
was intentional villainy. What the bad guys in movies did: mur-

der, torture, utterly unprompted meanness, monstrous acts as unreal as everything else in the movies. I had never intentionally set out to harm someone, and I didn't believe anyone else did either.

In my teenage years, I began to question the methods of stain removal thus far offered me. Three Hail Marys never reversed the original error, in my experience. I tried to feel the words when I prayed the Act of Contrition—"Oh my God, I am heartily sorry, for having offended Thee"[1]—but even feeling genuinely repentant didn't seem to make me any less likely to lie to my parents when I wanted to do something I knew they wouldn't allow or to attack my sisters if they were mean to me.

Bad behavior, I had come to believe by the time I entered college, simply evolved out of circumstances, chains of events. You said or did something; the other person took it wrong; you responded in some twisted, hurt way; the other person got mad; you got mad back; and so it continued until one or both of you did something really unfortunate that was never anyone's intention to begin with. That, in my thinking, was crime, borne out by all those statistics about the ills that so-called criminals had suffered—poverty, oppression, abuse—long before they ever committed their first crimes.

So, at twenty-three, on the eve of my assault, living in a city with one of the highest crime rates in the United States and armed with two college degrees but little experience of how things actually went in the world, I believed that crime was a series of harmless mistakes gone awry. Unintentional. Blameless. And I saw myself as the product of a history rife with the inequities and abuses that caused crime, of a society that had begun by slaughtering Indians and enslaving Africans and that continued, right up to the night of my assault, to marginalize certain groups—people who were different from the majority or who didn't speak English or who were for some other reason weaker than those in power. Any crimes that arose from such marginalizations were, to me, merely the natural consequences of society's failures. Society's *sins,* if you will. Crime at its worst—murder or war or capital punishment, which all amounted to the same thing to me—was, I firmly believed, society's fault, our collective fault and, by extension, *my* fault.

Thus, when a stranger tore the phone receiver from my hands in a public phone booth that night in December and, holding a gun to my head, sexually assaulted me while his buddy gathered up my purse and jewelry and book bag and kept a lookout so they didn't get caught, I was philosophically—as well as emotionally—at sea. If the criminals were themselves victims, I reasoned frantically, then someone else must have caused my suffering. As I saw it—as victims of sexual assault often see it—*I* was at fault, not my assaulters. And the police, who harped at me for using the phone booth late at night, and my family members and boyfriend, who didn't want me to talk about what had happened, and even my assaulters themselves didn't help me see it any differently.

"White girl, you like that," the one who touched me crooned, effectively transforming the crime into an act of retaliation for wrongs done by me and my white-girl ancestors.

As often happens after a crime or other tragedy, the following days brought attendant afflictions that loomed larger in my mind than the original event. First off, there was the agonizing response from everyone I knew that I "should be glad" I wasn't killed, that I was "lucky." It's hard to explain to someone how devastating such glib comforts can be in response to a rape or some other tragedy, but the title of Alice Sebold's account of her own rape, *Lucky*, references the universality of my pain.[2] To avoid it, I longed to retreat from my friends, my family, the world.

But my assaulters had my keys and IDs with my name and address on them, so I couldn't go home for weeks and had to live at a friend's house until I could get my locks replaced and burglar bars installed on all my windows. I was further immobilized by a crippling terror of going outside, especially out on the streets near my house or anywhere near the phone booth where the assault occurred. That meant that, since I didn't have a car and walked or rode my bike wherever I went, I didn't want to go anywhere at all. But I had classes to attend—both the three I was taking and the two I was teaching—and final grades to turn in and other end-of-semester errands to run, so I couldn't stay inside.

My students were angry when I explained, crying in front of them, that since all record of their semester's work had been lost in the assault, they would need to either show me the graded papers I had thus far given back and I would average them for a grade or else retype their final papers from their drafts, if they still had them. (In those days no one had a personal computer on which to save their work.) It was the last week of the semester. The students were scrambling to finish term papers for other courses while studying for finals and trying desperately to come up with ways to repair low grades in the last seconds before they went home for the holidays. In spirit, they were already far from school—eating Christmas dinner, opening presents, seeing friends and family they hadn't seen in months. The last thing they wanted was to rewrite a paper they hadn't cared about to begin with or scrounge around in their dorm rooms for scribbled-on papers they were pretty sure they had long since wadded up and thrown away. Their irritation with having to fit into their end-of-term frenzy what was essentially a big, new assignment—one they hadn't planned for—was completely understandable, even to me, but it upset me nonetheless and added to my growing sense that I was at fault in what had happened to me.

Meanwhile, I was worried about my own three papers: the fifty-page, end-of-semester productions expected of graduate students in English. Like my students, I had no copies saved, and all my notes and drafts had been in the book bag with the finished papers themselves. Without them I would have little to show for an entire semester's work.

When I went to the first professor to explain my situation, he didn't believe me and told me the paper was due on its due date, the last day before the Christmas holiday. The second professor gave me an extension until the beginning of spring semester, effectively eliminating my planned trip to Boston to see my boyfriend.

The third professor—a pale, white-haired professor emeritus who should long since have retired but stayed on by popular demand—taught Renaissance drama. It was an overlarge course, split between graduate students and undergraduates, but one of the most difficult courses I ever took. Despite dedicated preparation and emergency group study sessions, few of even us graduate students had been able to remember enough or read the plays with adequate insight to ace the midterm, and we all but despaired of writing fifty pages sufficiently original and smart to pique the professor's interest momentarily, much less impress him. I approached his office with special terror. When I told him what had happened, though, he cried—sobbed, actually, until I broke down too. We shared his box of tissues between us, not talking much. He wouldn't hear of my rewriting the paper.

"You have an A," he told me. His eyes were ringed with red. "Just forget about it."

It was a defining moment for me, spiritually speaking. Even though I had no belief whatsoever in God by then, it occurred to me nevertheless—some fond notion from my besotted Catholic childhood, as I explained it to myself—that this man was Jesus. That Jesus himself sat there with his dwindling supply of Kleenexes, not telling me I was lucky or should be glad when I was neither, but just crying for me, crying with me.

I don't remember that Christmas holiday at all—not where I ate Christmas dinner or if I received or gave any presents, certainly nothing of the birth underlying the season. That's not surprising, though. For the atheist I was in those days, Christmas was just red and green, tinsel, a turkey in the oven, carols, bells, cards sent and received. Even so, every December since that one, as the semester ratchets up into finals week and my students are getting cranky about their grades and the stores are full of Christmas, the miserable inheritance of those forgotten days—less the terror of the assault itself than the wretchedness that followed—overtakes me, and I enter a crippling, otherworldly gloom, a governing sadness I seem incapable of escaping, coupled with the sense of not being, or perhaps not wanting to be, part of this world. I can explain it no other way.

My mood is akin, I think, to what others have told me they experienced upon finding out they had a serious illness. They were utterly alone, they said, with the horrible knowledge. No other person—no friend, no matter how close, not even a spouse—could truly understand what they were feeling. They had a second-by-second awareness of time passing and a heightened consciousness of this world—its tiniest delights—yet at the same time an overwhelming sense of being outside of it already, not in it at all. Between earth and heaven, one of them told me. When I feel this way, my friends and even my husband and daughters seem far away from me. I long for them and simultaneously reject them.

I crave music then. Not my family's usual holiday music, but precisely the songs we hate, the ones in minor keys with melancholy tunes and lyrics. Interestingly, there are many such songs in the Christmas carol canon. "O Come, O Come, Emmanuel" comes immediately to mind, the quintessential hymn of Advent, a plea for release from tyranny, misery, death, darkness.[3] But there are so many others. "In the Bleak Midwinter," by the gloomily pious Christina Rossetti, for example, may be summed in one despondent phrase—"snow on snow, snow on snow"—a line that, despite my love of winter weather, just about captures the hopelessness I battle at this time of year.[4]

Longfellow's raw, near-despairing psalm, "I Heard the Bells on Christmas Day," is almost too bleak for even my most dejected mood. He wrote it on Christmas Day, 1864, in the midst of tragedies. The Civil War was raging, his soldier son had just arrived home from the front seriously wounded, and he was still sorely grieving the loss of his wife three years earlier. Her death had been particularly gruesome, and Longfellow probably blamed himself for it, to some degree. Her dress had caught on fire, and she had run to him for help, but he had been unable to extinguish the flames in time to save her. Christmases were especially hard for him after that, his journal entries attest. "Christmas Bells," as he called the poem that became the carol, reflects his struggle to reconcile his anguish with his faith. In the climax of the carol, the singer questions outright the gospel of Christmas, the angel's glad tidings of great joy:

And in despair I bowed my head;
"There is no peace on earth," I said;
"For hate is strong
and mocks the song
Of peace on earth, good-will to men."[5]

Longfellow goes on, as the biblical psalmists often do, to re-
nounce his own desperate, doubting words and rather precipi-
tously claim the hope that "God is not dead; nor doth he sleep!"
But it is the verse of despair that draws one—or, I should say,
that resonates with my own Christmastime despair, especially
in Pedro the Lion's slow, halting recording of the carol.[6]

Most years, one of these somber carols so grips me that I
have to listen to it over and over again—in the kitchen as I cook,
in the car, in my office at the university. I play the carol until my
daughters grow to despise it (and me, I suspect—their miserable Christmas-pooper of a mother) and until either they or my
husband makes me stop. Some years it is Amy Grant's "Breath
of Heaven," in which the confused, heavily pregnant mother of
God traveling to Bethlehem prays Grant's version of what has
become my own prayer when the despondency of Christmas
undoes me: Oh, dear heavenly Father, hold me together!

Recently the song was Sufjan Stevens's "Sister Winter," a
heartrending confession of failure to be grateful in all things, as
Paul often urges believers to be in his letters to the churches, to
comply with the additional Christmas mandate to be merry.[7]
The song expresses exactly my plight in the throes of Christmas

depression. The singer details the cause of his unhappiness—a love relationship gone bad in the past summer—and his efforts to be happy on his friends' behalf at Christmastime, but he nonetheless falls ever deeper into the song's plaintive center—"But my heart is returned to Sister Winter"—and the lamentation of the helplessly depressed: "I apologize, apologize." Despite my family's efforts, as we drive to the mall and deck the tree, to drown the song out with cheerier carols—Bing Crosby's drunken-sounding "Jingle Bells"[8] and Tom Waits's boogie-growling with the Blind Boys of Alabama to the good news carol, "Go Tell It on the Mountain"[9]—"Sister Winter" weeps on at the back of my mind: "But my heart is . . . apologize, apologize."

The year 2001 was an especially tough one for me. The World Trade Center attack somehow evoked the phone booth attack and brought the past slamming into the present in a full-blown case of post-traumatic stress disorder—in me characterized by alternating fits of terror, rage and crying—that has taken me years of subsequent therapy to learn to manage. My carol of choice that Christmas was James Taylor's coincidentally commemorative rendition of "Have Yourself a Merry Little Christmas" (he actually recorded it before 9/11), in which he subverts the optimism of the famous Frank Sinatra version by replacing shining stars on boughs with the song's darker original lyrics about muddling through somehow.[10] I listened to Taylor's grief-cracked voice, and muddled, and cried.

One Christmas season the song I craved was not a Christmas song at all but raw-voiced Natalie Merchant singing the anonymous folk song—or slave spiritual, perhaps, as some scholars speculate—"I Am a Poor Wayfaring Stranger."[11] The words, in case you have never grieved them into your consciousness as I have, are relentlessly dark, expressing a longing for something better so insistent it seems remembered, a corporeal urge built into us creatures of God for the opposite of what we see around us: the opposite of evil, the opposite of pain, the opposite of loss and despair. The poor wayfaring stranger keens, it seems to me, for the loss of what might have been, had our world not become, as the writer of Genesis describes it, "corrupt in God's sight" (Genesis 6:11). What might have been if the world were not, as God himself explained to Noah, so "filled with violence" because of the humans he had created that he was obliged to destroy them (Genesis 6:13).

In Natalie Merchant's "Poor Wayfaring Stranger,"[12] the "bright bright land" toward which she makes her wandering way is an evanescent vision, more dreamed than actually glimpsed in the distance. The singer's attention lingers instead on the very miseries she seeks to escape. "I am a poor, wayfaring stranger / Traveling through this world of woe," she wails, then takes us through an orphaned life of "sickness . . . toil . . . danger . . . trials" and "self-denial," a lonely roaming of ways "rough and steep," surrounded by "dark clouds," and ending finally "in the old church yard." A dark song at Christmastide if there ever was one, offering only a few spots of cheer, all of them vague to the point of being almost invisible: a dimly remembered dead mother and other nameless "loved ones" waiting for her "over

Jordan," an equally hazy "Savior," and the "beautiful fields" of a home she's never seen, peopled by "God's redeemed."

The elusive heaven we all long for, the wayfaring stranger hopes on our behalf, is a place to which we belong, our home. It wasn't that hope that captured my mood in the song, though, during that Christmas when I played it again and again and watched, again and again, the two glimmering towers collapsing into ashes and bits of paper. Rather it was my growing realization that evil existed. Genuine evil, intended and inescapable. That we are all perpetrators of it, yes, just as we are all its victims.

The Christmas of 2001—ironically a Christmas that came on the ashy heels of the worst news I had ever watched on television or listened to on the radio or read about in the papers—was my introduction to what the "good news" of the angels really meant: namely, that God had offered—was offering still—a solution to the violence with which we humans fill the world to this day. Glad tidings. Great joy. The birth of Jesus is *that* good news, I realized for the first time.

It is interesting to consider that, in suffering the consequences of evil, we share the experience of Jesus—not only in his suffering on the cross, but also in his suffering from the first moment of birth. Having "emptied himself out" to become human, as the nativity hymn Paul cites in Philippians 2 attests, Baby Jesus surely wasn't aware of the life of torment he was embarking on. But consider: He was born to parents unable to find or perhaps even to afford a decent room and cast into a world so unwelcoming as to offer a woman about to give birth no more comfortable shelter than a dirty stable. Jesus' first objections to the pain of entry into this world of woe, his first baby whimpers, were heard by no one but his fellow sufferers. His first bed was a feed trough. From babyhood Jesus was already the victim of aggression, with a price on his head so extreme that other Jewish babies would be killed to find him. His earliest memories were probably of fleeing to Egypt with his family, refugees from violence.

Jesus knew firsthand what it was to be a poor, wayfaring stranger. He chose to be one, it occurred to me that Christmas as I listened to the song again and again. His first baby cries, I decided, would have had that knowledge in them too. The wayfarer's grim knowledge of this world's corruption and violence.

Jesus suffered all the pains of our world—not only the normal human discomforts of being squeezed through a birth canal and then plopped out cold and helpless to gulp his first lungfuls of our world's harsh air, but the special distresses and indignities of the poor and rejected: being dirty and uncomfortable, hungry, homeless, outcast, lonely. In the course of his life he was hated and attacked, rejected, mocked, even forsaken by his own Father as he died. Long before the events of the Passion, Jesus and his friends got so hungry they had to pluck grain from someone's field to fill their bellies. On another occasion Jesus commented wryly to a would-be follower, "Foxes have dens and birds have nests, but the Son of Man has no place to lay his head" (Luke 9:58).

Standing at the grave of his friend Lazarus and confronted by Lazarus's mourning, accusing sisters—"Lord, if you had been here, my brother would not have died," they each complain (John 11:21, 32)—Jesus stuns us with his humanness by grieving the loss he was about to restore. "Jesus wept," his best friend John reports (11:35). God wept! And he would weep again, looking down on Jerusalem—ironically, the City of Peace—and contemplating the violence of God's children and his own impending death:

> Jerusalem, Jerusalem, you who kill the prophets and stone those sent to you, how often I have longed to gather your children together, as a hen gathers her chicks under her wings, and you were not willing. Look, your house is left to you desolate. I tell you, you will not see me again until you say, "Blessed is he who comes in the name of the Lord." (Luke 13:34-35)

Jesus' tears for us move me. He is a fellow sufferer, the victim of human evil, soon to be one of the very prophets he speaks of here, who were killed for their words of warning, and yet he mourns the desolation to be suffered by the human perpetrators of these evils. He mourns our desolation, that is, both as doers of evil and as its inevitable victims. But it occurred to me that Christmas—the Christmas following September 11, 2001, a Christmas when I did little else but cry—that Jesus had cried from birth. Indeed, the first words of Jesus—the first words of "the Word," as John calls him in his Gospel (1:1)—were a baby's cries of woe.

I find odd comfort in the knowledge that we worship a God who cries. Cries as babies cry in that moment of birth—in terror and pain, in shock, in hunger, in need of reassurance. God cries for our loss and pain, as that professor cried for mine, surrounded by books and papers and empty Kleenex boxes. And God cries in frustration and love and hope for us, surely, as Jesus cried for the inhabitants of Jerusalem.

God cries not only for us—and about us and with us—but for himself, I think. Certainly Jesus did. In Gethsemane, where he is so "deeply distressed and troubled" that he tells his companions, "My soul is overwhelmed with sorrow to the point of death" (Mark 14:33-34). And later, on the cross, he "cried out in a loud voice, . . . 'My God, my God, why have you forsaken me?'" (Matthew 27:46). Moments later, mocked in his agony, he "cried out again in a loud voice" even as he "gave up his spirit" (Matthew 27:50). I suppose one might argue that Jesus only cries as the Son of Man and not in his divine capacity as part of the Trinity. But Paul tells us that the Holy Spirit "intercedes for us through wordless groans" (Romans 8:26). I believe that God the Father—the Most High, the Creator, Yahweh—cries, too. Just as I cried before my students that day in class, God mourns his own unmerited suffering at our hands. He cries out of the relentless love that his messed-up children routinely spurn. He suffers our violence to one another so extremely, the writer of Genesis reports, that he regrets having made us and experiences pain. God the Father suffered, and surely continues to suffer, on our behalf.

He surely cries for joy too, though. I'm guessing he cried at the birth of his Son, as any of us would. And he will cry at the reunion we will one day experience—for him it is now—when we finally return home, where we belong. Perhaps he will sing with us then, simultaneously remembering his past pain and celebrating his present joy, the sad-happy song I listened to during my season of sorrow: "I'm only going over Jordan! I'm only going over home."

12

SEEKING GOD

Early on in what I might call the advent of my adult faith, when my first unsettling recognitions of truth had yet to metamorphose into a confident acceptance of Jesus as God and the Bible as God's message to his children, a woman in a Bible study class I was attending startled me with the audacious statement that if she'd been a Jew of Jesus' time, she would have dropped everything and followed him. She was certain. It was that clear from the writings of the prophets and from David's psalms, she said, that Jesus was the Messiah.

Although the woman's self-assurance impressed me, I was skeptical. First off, I'm always skeptical when people say they know what they would have done in some hypothetical situation. I know from abundant past experiences that I rarely manage to behave as I would like to think I would. Looking back on the sexual assault of my twenties, for example, it seems to me as though my body acted entirely independently from how the version of me that survived to tell the story would have liked. With a gun to my head, I became a different person than I was even then and certainly than the person I have become since that time. I stood silent, compliant, calm almost— or, anyway, utterly emotionless and automatic in my responses, like a robot. As in my worst dreams, I lost the ability to cry out, but I had no real urge to scream. I resisted my attackers only briefly, vaguely, when they grabbed at the heavy book bag that held my students' and my work for the semester. And when it was all over and my attackers were already halfway down the street, when the terror and humiliation of the assault were all but past and I was safe, I suddenly found my voice and called the men back to me.

"You forgot my earrings," I chirped into the darkness. I held out the small gold earrings they had told me to remove. One of them ran back, grabbed the earrings, and ran away again, hissing, "Don't scream or I'll shoot you!"

I'm sure they laughed about it afterward.

"She called us back!" I imagined them crowing to their friends.

Only after decades of shame can I even tell this part of the story openly. I was complicit with my enemies. I participated in my own assault. My silence and nonresistance may have saved me, as everyone has pointed out since, but, paradoxically, I knew I had aided in my own devastation. Even now twenty-some years later, despite my therapist's revelation that under threat of death our bodies legitimately shut down in order to spare us pain—that it's not uncommon for crime victims to assist perpetrators in their unconscious effort to stay alive—I still feel ashamed when I consider those earrings and my rediscovered voice calling my attackers back. These memories have become the emblem of my powerlessness to act as I would have liked—to have resisted or screamed or at least been willing to fight for my life.

As a consequence of this experience and many others, whenever people tell me, "I know what I would have done"—when they boast, as someone inevitably does in a conversation about the Holocaust, for example, "I know I would never have looked away while my neighbors were rounded up like livestock and packed off to work camps with tall smokestacks filling the air with black ash"—I cringe internally for them, for their future shame when they discover that they might fail themselves, as I did, in a crisis.

The disconnect between what we want to do and what we do, I have come to believe, pretty much defines us as humans. The stories of those who knew Jesus during his lifetime provide many examples. Jesus' disciples, who witnessed miracles, are terrified in the storm as Jesus lies sleeping. They fall asleep instead of praying in Gethsemane. Simon Peter, who has witnessed miracle upon miracle as well as the transfiguration and confidently proclaimed to Jesus, "You are the Messiah, the Son of the living God" (Matthew 16:16), nevertheless fails this same Messiah just as he is being hauled off to be tortured and killed. In short, Jesus' most intimate acquaintances and devoted followers, the men and women who will establish his church after his death and resurrection, seem incapable of acting in accordance with their faith.

Even Paul, who went to prison and ultimately died for following Jesus, admits to this problem. "What I want to do I do not do, but what I hate I do," he laments at length in his letter to the Romans (7:15). "I have the desire to do what is good, but I cannot carry it out. For I do not do the good I want to do, but the evil I do not want to do—this I keep on doing" (Romans 7:18-19). The others in my Bible study class were always pointing out to me evidence of Paul's absolute uprightness and acuity in matters of faith, but it was this sorry admission—that Paul, like me, *never* succeeded in doing what he wanted to do—that won him as a model for me. "What a wretched man I am!" he exclaims finally. "Who will rescue me from this body of death?" (Romans 7:24 TNIV). Who indeed!

Our inevitable failure to do as we think we will in a hypothetical situation was, however, not the only reason I doubted my friend's professed ability to have recognized the promised Messiah in the flesh. There's plenty of evidence in Scripture that seeing does not, contrary to popular opinion, necessarily lead to believing. Jesus tells the story of a rich man in hell who begs Abraham to send the beggar Lazarus, who used to lie at the gate of his mansion and is now in heaven, to warn his brothers so that they won't share his fate. Abraham refuses, commenting that even seeing someone sent back from the dead won't convince some people—which, of course, proves all too true when Jesus reappears after his own death. Jesus' closest friends, whom he had told on several occasions that he would die and rise again, struggle to believe it's really him upon his return from the grave.

The woman in my Bible study class, although clearly a believer, reminded me of the escaped convict called the Misfit in one of my favorite short stories, "A Good Man Is Hard to Find" by Flannery O'Connor.[1] The Misfit murders a family whose car has broken down on the side of the road. Just before he shoots the last remaining family member—an old grandmother who keeps chattering on about how, if he'd pray, Jesus would help him be a good person—he muses that he wishes he had been alive when Jesus was because then he'd know for sure if Jesus' claims were true and he wouldn't be the kind of person he was. If he had personally witnessed Jesus raising people from the dead, the Misfit says, almost crying, he'd have known who Jesus was and would have followed him.

Statistically speaking, the Misfit probably would *not* have recognized Jesus as God's Son even if he had seen him perform miracles. Many of Jesus' contemporaries didn't recognize him as the Messiah, and some of them—certainly the Pharisees and priests and teachers of the law who were always heckling him—

probably knew the relevant messianic passages of Scripture better than anyone in my Bible study class did. It was the custom for religiously inclined Jewish boys to memorize the entire Law and the Prophets, we had been learning. Educated Jews of Jesus' time knew the prophecies of the Messiah, if anyone did, but they still rejected him when he came.

"Why do you think *you* would have been any different?" I asked the woman in my Bible study class.

I didn't tell her the real reason I was suspicious of her claim. It was a reason that seemed too dangerous to voice in those days, when I was on the very brink of faith. In truth, I'm still a little disturbed by this particular doubt among the many upon which my faith makes its wobbly stand. It is this: The whole time we were studying the Old Testament prophecies of the coming of the Messiah—that a virgin would give birth, that it would happen in Bethlehem, that the child would be called Immanuel, that he would bring honor to Galilee, that his hands and feet and side would be pierced but his bones not broken, that everything would be different when he came—I kept thinking, *Who in the world would ever have expected any of these verses to come true? Who would have ever sorted precisely these details from the thousands of similarly specific statements and names and places that fill the pages of the Old Testament?*

The messianic passages seemed prophetic to me only in hindsight. I hardly dared to allow myself this doubt; I was that near to believing in spite of it. Even so, it colored every prophetic claim I heard, whether it was the Gospel writers' assertions that this or that happened in fulfillment of Scripture or Jesus himself saying, as he does on a few occasions, "This Scripture is talking about me." He tells a group of Pharisees and rabbis looking for a sign, for example, that his death was prophesied in this sentence from the book of Jonah: "Now the LORD provided a huge fish to swallow Jonah, and Jonah was in the belly of the fish three days and three nights" (Jonah 1:17). Read in context, the sentence appears to pertain only to Jonah's story, not some future event. Who would ever have imagined, without Jesus specifically saying so, that the detail would have anything at all to do with the fact that Jesus would spend "three days and three nights in the heart of the earth" (Matthew 12:40)?

The nature of prophecy—the whole metaphorical, metaphysical, metastatic indirection of its linkages—flummoxed me as a new believer. Given the layering of biblical prophecies and the way they had of referring to events in the biblical writer's time as well as the coming birth and death and resurrection of Jesus and also future events that have yet to happen, how did the readers of Jesus' time know which stories were prophetic and which weren't? In the pandemonium of battles and captivities and migrations they endured, how did they know which events had already happened—which people had already been overthrown, which lands claimed, which sins repaid—and which would happen at some later date? How did anyone know even to expect a Messiah in the first place? A real person of their own acquaintance who, as Isaiah improbably asserted, would "wipe away the tears from all faces," "destroy the shroud that enfolds all peoples," and "swallow up death forever" (Isaiah 25:7-8)? What exactly did it mean, even to people of Jesus' time, that an anointed one—whether David's son, as he's called in some passages, or God With Us, as he's called in others—would save them? By what trick of thinking did they manage to sort their fantasies from God's actual promises?

It is amazing to me that we recognize Jesus as the Messiah at all, even in retrospect. Even with New Testament writers reminding us—writing fifty, seventy, a hundred years after Jesus' resurrection and return to heaven—of indistinct prophetic Old Testament passages that supposedly prefigured the story of Jesus' arrival on earth. And most prophecies foundational to the Christian faith, mind you, have not yet discernibly occurred. We still die. The lion—the more scripturally correct wolf, for that matter—still devours the lamb. Rest seems to remain unattainable, despite scriptural promises that Jesus will bring it, that he himself *is* our rest. How does it happen that we are ever able to snag hold of a scriptural passage about the future with which to substantiate our faith here, now, today?

The nature of faith fascinates me. Confounds me. I think, on the one hand, that it is not something one can create through reason and logic, or even through the most obvious similarities between what one forgotten writer said and what actually came to pass. Genuine faith should not be something I can simply convince myself of. I have convinced myself of many seeming truths over the years, and then I have changed my mind. Truth, as we know it in this world, can be variously defended. Indeed, my field of writing, otherwise known as rhetoric, is all about convincing oneself and others of arguable truths. Real truth, I believed in those days when I was entering faith and even in the years of atheism that preceded them, must be something else. Something beyond arguments and proofs. Real truth—and, by extension, real faith—must come directly from God.

Jesus praises the faith of small children, who have surely expended no effort to attain it. He also asserts, "No one can come to me unless the Father who sent me draws them" (John 6:44). That is what seemed to happen to me when, midway through a lifetime, I became a believer. Suddenly, all the arguments, all the evidence, all knowledge, all my doubts fell away, and I felt myself simply drawn.

There are, on the other hand, all those biblical injunctions to believe, as if believing were something I could *choose* to do. All those calls to turn and see God and have greater faith. Jesus repeatedly condemns the "little faith" of his followers when they didn't trust God to take care of them (Matthew 6:30; 8:26; 14:31; 16:8; 17:20; Luke 12:28). On one occasion he extends his hand to Thomas and tells him, "Put your finger here; see my hands. Reach out your hand and put it into my side. Stop doubting and believe" (John 20:27). All of Scripture, it seems to me, is one long call either to have faith or to have more of it than one has—and as such it is an argument that faith involves some sort of action on our part.

For these reasons, of all the stories of Christmas, the story of the wise men following a star to find Jesus especially intrigues me. Like all stories of coming to God, it is at its core untellable, and Matthew, the only Gospel writer who undertook to tell it, leaves out many crucial details. Who were these men from the East, exactly? How, as foreigners, did they even know about a promised Savior to the Jews to begin with? Did they find what they were expecting when they went in search of a recently born "king of the Jews" whom they wanted to worship (Matthew 2:2)? Why did they link a star and the coming of this king? What was different about the star they saw rise from all the other stars in the heavens? How did they come to recognize it as *Jesus'* star?

These wise men traveled faithfully from their distant home to "the place where the child was," Matthew writes, and "when they saw the star, they were overjoyed" (Matthew 2:9-10). Why were they suddenly so happy? Had they perhaps lost sight of the star and become worried that their searching had been in vain? The star moved and led them and seemed to have the ability— unlike any star or comet or meteor I have ever seen—to indicate a place. How was that so? Was it actually a star at all? These are all mysteries the story does not deign to resolve.

We are told the men were "magi"—the plural of *magus*, a word that comes to us via Greek from the Old Persian word *maguš*, which means "priest" or "mighty one." Our words *might* and *mighty* share the same Indo-European root. *Magus* is also the source of our modern words *magic* and *magician*. In the account of the magi in Matthew, the word is usually translated as "wise men," but elsewhere in the New Testament the same Greek

word is routinely translated as "sorcerer." In Acts, Luke re-
counts the story of a sorcerer named Simon, referred to among
early Christians as Simon Magus. He practiced sorcery that
"amazed all the people of Samaria" (Acts 8:9), was called "Great
Power of God" (Acts 8:10), and eventually came, we're told, to
believe Philip's teaching of "the good news of the kingdom of
God and the name of Jesus Christ" (Acts 8:12) and be baptized. Later, though, Simon the Sorcerer tried to buy from Peter and John the ability to lay hands on people to invoke the
Holy Spirit, a clearly mercenary act—subsequently called *simony*,
in reference to him—that casts his motives if not the authentic-
ity of his faith into question. Later in Acts, Luke writes of another magus, the "Jewish sorcerer and false prophet named
Bar-Jesus," or Son of Jesus, whom Paul accuses of being "full of
all kinds of deceit and trickery" (13:6, 10). Paul calls on God to
blind Bar-Jesus for "perverting the right ways of the Lord"
(Acts 13:10). Magi, in other words, hardly seem the likeliest
people to be among the first believers to worship Jesus.

Scholars describe the original magi of pre-Islamic Persia as
cultic priests, possibly Zoroastrians. The early Greek historian
Herodotus, writing about four centuries before Jesus' birth,
described magi as Median priests responsible for sacrifices and
interpretations of signs. Persian leaders in those days consulted
magi to elucidate upsetting dreams and to aid in decision-
making, much as kings in the Old Testament—even kings who
did not worship the one true God—consulted the Jewish
prophets. Herodotus's account often represents the Medians in

general and the magi in particular as shockingly brutal. In one passage, Herodotus remarks,

> The Magi are a very peculiar race, different entirely from the Egyptian priests, and indeed from all other men whatsoever. The Egyptian priests make it a point of religion not to kill any live animals except those which they offer in sacrifice. The Magi, on the contrary, kill animals of all kinds with their own hands, except dogs and men. They even seem to take a delight in the employment, and kill, as readily as they do other animals, ants and snakes, and such like flying and creeping things.[2]

As a Median-Persian subject himself, Herodotus may have been somewhat biased in his representation of magi. By New Testament times, the term *magi*—although used disparagingly to refer to sorcerers and defrauders by early Christians, as we have seen—had likely come to refer neutrally to all sorts of cultic priests or itinerant prophets claiming special powers.

From the biblical account in Matthew, in any case, we can assume that the magi who visited the Christ child studied the sky. In fact, some translations of the Bible (Wycliffe,[3] Amplified,[4] *Hoffnung für Alle*[5]) refer to the magi as astrologers. How the magi managed to interpret what they saw, though—whether by the same deceptions as Simon the Sorcerer and Bar-Jesus— we are not told. I like to think of them simply as genuinely "wise" men—that is, not merely learned or intelligent men but men who were paying attention to creation, which, as Paul writes in Romans, provides all the evidence we need of who God is. Unlike those who are "without excuse" (Romans 1:20) and given over to their own depravity and ultimate destruction, the magi apparently not only recognized God in creation but sought to worship him. They searched the sky and probably the rest of "what has been made" (Romans 1:20) for evidence of "what may be known about God" (Romans 1:19), and they went after it. The magi who followed that star were, in other words, active seekers of God.

But how did they know that the star they saw would lead them to God—or even, as they called him, to a newborn king of the Jews whom they wanted to worship? Perhaps they didn't. Perhaps their understanding of the star's portent developed only as they sought it. Perhaps, at the outset, they were simply captivated by the unusual moving star and followed it out of sheer, childlike delight for its beauty and uniqueness.

Once, when Charlotte and Lulu were toddlers, we saw a fabulous rainbow. It was a rare complete one: Both sides of the arc were not only visible but looked solid, like two brilliant, glassy stanchions rising from the brown trees in the distance to form a clear arch against the sky. The girls begged to go "through the rainbow," and, for a lark, I let them think that this was possible. We got in the car and made our way in that direction.

We drove and drove. It was their naptime—another motivation for a car trip. They typically resisted sleep, and I sometimes resorted to tricking them into napping by driving around the countryside until they nodded off and then carried their sleep-heavy bodies to their beds. But they didn't nod off this time. Far from it. They stayed alert, pointed, gave me baby directions whenever the lay of the roads took us off track. We drove and drove and drove. The girls still remember that fruitless journey—the tangible-seeming columns of color, the excitement of the seeking, their disappointment when the afternoon started to darken and the rainbow to fade away. They cried when I said we had to go home.

Perhaps the magi's journey was like the rainbow search for my daughters: the excited pursuit of God's invisible qualities—his power, his creativity, his bizarre love—so abundantly displayed in what he had made. "Where is the one who has been born king of the Jews?" the magi asked wherever they went. "We saw his star when it rose and have come to worship him" (Matthew 2:2). Later, after answering the worried summons of the sitting king of the Jews, they saw the star again and were "overjoyed" (Matthew 2:10), the English word here but a sober substitute for the clot of words used in the Greek: two words meaning "great" and two more meaning "extreme joy." Other versions capture a bit better the magi's response to rediscovering the star: "When they saw the star," the King James Version reads, "they rejoiced with exceeding great joy." William Tyndale, writing in 1526, has them "marvelously glad."[6] In the Amplified Bible, "they were thrilled with ecstatic joy." And in my favorite translation of the passage, from Wycliffe's Bible of 1382, they "joyed with a full great joy." There was something about that star, in other words, that electrified those magi. I'm thinking that the magi were motivated, in part at least, by simple enthusiasm for the star itself—for the magnificence of God's creation—and that their journey in pursuit of the star, like my daughters' rainbow quest, was one of pure delight.

T. S. Eliot would not think so. In his famous poetic rendering of the magi passage in Matthew, "The Journey of the Magi," the wise men did not share my daughters' breathless enthusiasm for the journey, even though, unlike Charlotte and Lulu, they did eventually arrive. In Eliot's telling, the journey itself was difficult and unpleasant. A sacrifice, not an embrace, of earth's delights. Eliot's wise men are certainly more subdued than my daughters and I would have been had we managed to enter the world beyond that rainbow. Of finding the Christ child, the speaker—one magus, looking back on the journey— comments only that it was "satisfactory."

Eliot wrote "The Journey of the Magi" just after being baptized, and his poem, though ostensibly about the magi's expedition, simultaneously traces his own conversion to Christianity and Jesus' earthly journey from birth to death. The poem opens in bleakest winter, and the magus dwells not on the discovery but on what he and his fellow magi have had to give up to make the journey—and on the miseries of the trip itself. Coming to faith, Eliot thus argues in the voice of a brand new believer, is an unpleasant undertaking, involving sacrifice and hardship.

Eliot borrows the opening words of his poem almost verbatim from a sermon on the magi preached on Christmas Day in

1622 at Whitehall Palace, with King James in attendance, by Lancelot Andrewes, then Bishop of Winchester, an early Anglican father whose writings Eliot was studying at the time of his conversion[7]:

> A cold coming they had of it this time of the year, just the worst time of year to take a journey, and specially a long journey. The ways deep, the weather sharp, the days short, the sun farthest off, *in solsitio burmali,* "the very dead of winter."

Andrewes was a regular preacher to first Queen Elizabeth and then King James and had been one of forty-seven scholars appointed to work on the King James Version of the Bible, of which he is believed to have functioned as project overseer. Firmly Protestant in his theology, he nonetheless defended continuity with the church's past and traditions, including such practices as making the sign of the cross, regarded as "popish" by his contemporaries and thus risky to support in those violent times. Andrewes's sermons were ornate and scholarly, and he frequently used the Latin of his education (and Roman Catholicism) in lieu of the plain English that had by then become the language of the English church. Paradoxically, Andrewes was also attracted to the Puritans of his time, esteeming especially their adherence to Scripture, their pursuit of a personal relationship with Jesus and their dedication to holy living. In the end, though, he faulted the Puritans, according to Davidson R. Morse, for neglecting "God's self-giving, his coming, dwelling, and living the human experience" and failing "to grasp the mystery of the Incarnation."[8] Given these sentiments, Andrewes wrote frequently on the subject of Jesus' birth.

In the Christmas sermon Eliot references in his poem, Andrewes focuses on the magi's perspective and, like Eliot, reads their story as the story of coming to faith. He stresses the words *see* and *come*—*vidimus* and *venimus* in Latin (we have seen and we have come)—in the opening lines of Matthew's account: "Where is he that is born King of the Jews? for we have seen his star in the east, and are come to worship him" (Matthew 2:2 KJV). As in one of my favorite Christmas carols, "Adeste fideles" ("O Come, All Ye Faithful"),[9] Andrewes sees the "good news" of Christmas—proclaimed by the angels to the shepherds and lived out by the magi—as above all a call to come. "It was but *vidimus, venimus*, with them," Andrewes preached; "they saw, and they came." He urged his listeners to experience faith in the same way. It repeatedly struck me in reading Andrewes's sermon how the advent of Jesus necessitates other "advents": the coming of the shepherds to the manger, the coming of the magi to the house where the Jewish child-king lived, the coming of believers to faith.

In Eliot's poem and even more so in Andrewes's retelling and analysis of the magi's story, we are imaginatively transported to an icy-sounding place and season much like what London must have been like the day Andrewes preached his sermon. Such a setting is probably incorrect, geographically and meteorologically speaking, yet powerful in its underlying message, which informs both Andrewes's sermon and Eliot's poem: faith requires dedicated seeking, an immediate coming in response to seeing, heedless of obstacles. The magi's journey to Jesus, Andrewes concludes, was "a wearisome, irksome, troublesome, dangerous, unseasonable journey," but they came "cheerfully and quickly."

They also came asking everyone where he was. "*Venerunt dicentes,*" Andrewes stresses: "They came with it in their mouths"—in other words, as Andrewes says, "confessing Him boldly." Although the magi were foreigners unlikely to be welcomed in that place and perhaps even in danger for their lives among a people who had once been captives in the magi's own country, they "spake of it so freely, to so many, as it came to Herod's ear." So too Andrewes exhorts his royal audience—and Eliot and us several hundred years later—to approach God: openly seeking, unembarrassed to ask for directions and determined to get there, whatever the risk. We shouldn't just "sit still as we say, and let nature work," he emphasizes. We have to *seek* faith. "Set down this," Andrewes concludes emphatically, using a phrase that Eliot will steal for his poem three hundred years later: "to find where He is, we must learn to ask where He is" and then join the generation described in Psalm 24 "of them that seek Him."

I find it strange that Christians these days use the word *seeker* in reference to someone who is not yet a believer. When I question generally held beliefs of my faith, other Christians often perceive me as doubting them, if not challenging them outright. Believers, such Christians seem to imply, should be done seeking. They should have found out all the answers and be done asking questions. For Andrewes, and for me, the initial call to faith and the subsequent call to greater faith amount to the same thing: We must keep on asking where God is, keep on seeking him.

That's what the magi were, I think. Not sorcerers or priests or men of any particular might. Not expounders of mysteries, not hierophants with the answers, not even confident knowers of the whole truth of the birth, but humble seekers who pursued wisdom and knowledge of God by observing, asking questions and struggling to understand.

There were many such magi—questioners, doubters, seekers—among the first Christians. "Lord, where are you going?" Peter asks not long before the cock crows. "Lord, why can't I follow you now?" (John 13:36-37). And consider the old Pharisee Nicodemus, whom Jesus calls "Israel's teacher" (John 3:10). Struggling, seeking, on the very brink of believing, Nicodemus demands, "How can someone be born when they are old? . . . Surely they cannot enter a second time into their mother's womb to be born!" (John 3:4). Even after Jesus explains, the wise old man keeps on asking, "How can this be?" (John 3:9). I envision Nicodemus in eternity, basking in the complete knowledge denied us in this world, seeking still—asking, although in the presence of the all-sufficient Answer.

I don't know what I would have done if I had met Jesus in his time on earth. I would like to think, like the woman in my first Bible study class, that I would have recognized him as the Messiah. Or at least as someone with special wisdom. It is pleasant to imagine that I would have sat spellbound at his feet like his friend Mary. Or that I would have had even the lesser faith of her sister Martha, who merely cooked meals for Jesus and his followers and cleaned up afterward and complained but who, in a crisis of grief and despair at their brother's tomb and frustrated that Jesus had not come in time to heal Lazarus as he had healed so many others, could nevertheless stalwartly confess, when Jesus questions her faith, "I believe that you are the Messiah, the Son of God, who is to come into the world" (John 11:27). It would be nice to believe that my spirit, unlike those of Peter and James and John, would not have caved to my flesh in the garden of Gethsemane, as it did when I was assaulted—that I would have managed to keep watch over Jesus while he prayed, or that I would have sought if not *his* protection against the enemies watching from the distance, at least my own. That would have been (to use Eliot's word) more than satisfactory.

For now, though, it is enough to keep on seeking. To see the star—that came, that comes yet—and to wonder, and to stumble, stupidly, after it.

13

LIVING LIFE
ABUNDANTLY

A Parable

Every year, usually on the first day of the official Christmas season, the day after Thanksgiving, my husband and I take an overnight trip to the big mall in Tulsa—or, if it's been a prosperous year, to Kansas City—to do our Christmas shopping. Nowadays, we mostly buy presents for each other on this trip, since our daughters are at the age of wanting mostly either clothes they pick out themselves or else CDs or electronic items that we order on the Internet. Back when Charlotte and Lulu were little, though, we devoted these buying sprees entirely to strategizing how to please them.

In truth, we bought mostly what appealed to us. Kris favored the remote-control cars, board books and ant farms of his childhood. On one trip, we searched everywhere for rockets with electric igniters that he said he and the girls would set off out in the field when the weather got warmer. I wanted to buy them all the girly toys in the Sears catalog that I had longed for as a child but that I never got because my parents had determined early on that I was to be a scientist. Talking dolls. Miniature tea sets. A rock tumbler with which to produce the raw ingredients of sparkly rings and bracelets. A cotton candy maker. An Easy-Bake Oven and a huge assortment of mixes to go with it. Christmas shopping was a gratifying task in those days, sweetened simultaneously by the fulfillment—though by proxy—of past longings and the anticipated thrill of our daughters' pleasure on Christmas morning. Even in years when we should have been careful with our money, we came home loaded down with bags and boxes.

As soon as we got home, before picking up the girls from their grandmother's house and taking them home to bed, we stashed all the presents away in the high places of our closets and next to the heating duct beneath the stairs. While we worked—Kris up on the ladder making space and me down below handing things up to him—we discussed how we'd have to clear space for the new toys in our daughters' rooms and in their affections by getting rid of toys from previous years. Toys they no longer played with or never had. Toys they were too old for and some other child might want. Toys they'd had when they were babies. Toys that were missing pieces and could no longer be used as they were intended. Toys that were scattered everywhere or piled up in baskets or tubs according to size or type or the material they were made of or some equally feckless principle of organization. Kris called it "getting rid of all the junky plastic."

"Let's get rid of some of these old toys you guys don't play with anymore," I coaxed the girls the next morning, reluctant from experience to just gather things up and toss them without first consulting their owners. By way of example, I held up an orange plastic cylinder that used to go in the circle hole of a shape sorter we got for Charlotte way before she was even able to sit up and see it. From where I stood, I could see one of its companion pieces, a lime green triangle, under her bed. The toy's cube-shaped frame was no longer with us, having sojourned for some years out in the sand box before our dog Richard chewed it apart and then sowed its bright blue pieces in sunny spots all over the yard.

"But that's our dolls' vomino bowl," Charlotte told me, grabbing the orange cylinder out of my hand. *Vomino* was the girls' baby word for vomit. She stooped to put the vomit bowl on the counter, near the stainless steel sink, of a Barbie-sized kitchen island.

"What about these?" I asked, dumping a broken basket of plastic animals out on the bed in a bright pile. There were little pink and green and blue dinosaurs, various bugs about the same size in biologically correct colors, a collection of fictional creatures from McDonald's Happy Meals, a tiny farmer from Kris's youth, and a number of cattle—some missing legs or parts of their heads—that had been in a lawn mower accident the previous summer.

"It's our army," Lulu declared, appearing from nowhere like a camouflaged soldier from behind a tree that hadn't been there the day before. She was wearing Charlotte's old princess dress together with gigantic black Darth Vader athletic shoes, and she carried a plastic pirate's sword we got at Disneyland one year.

"Well, I'm throwing that away," I said menacingly, pointing at a pet-sized tiger, another of Kris's old toys, which was losing stuffing all over the floor. The large cavity in its belly used to contain a nonfunctional mechanical part that I surmised was probably lying around somewhere too. Lulu threw her body across the tiger before I could get there, and Charlotte told me it just needed to be sewn up.

We continued this way for about an hour before I gave up and started to go away, having wrested from them an exploded-looking shoebox, two stretched-out rubber bands, a few capless markers and an old rhinestone earring missing most of its stones that used to belong to me anyway. The girls, by this time, were playing happily, making use of every item we'd discussed in a merry parade of dolls and dinosaurs and stuffed animals and little plastic monkeys linked hand to hand that stretched all the way from the door of Lulu's room down the hall to the bathroom and, via the damp purple bathmat, up and over and into the bathtub—which, they told me, was Westville, the town where we live.

That weekend was the Westville Christmas parade, a paltry assemblage of homemade floats and burnt turkey drumsticks and locals hawking used items left over from their fall garage sales. We'd never attended the parade, but the girls had heard about it from their friends and imagined it as something akin to their definition of heaven: where everything was sweet and fun and dead pets came back to life.

"You won't have any room for all the new stuff you might get for Christmas," I reminded them sternly, sadly, from the bathroom door.

"That's okay," Charlotte told me. She was dancing a three-legged cow up the purple mat and didn't bother, not even at the magic word *Christmas,* to turn all the way around to speak to me. At that moment she was looking not ahead to all the good things to come but regarding with fierce excitement what she already had, what she held in her very hand.

Ⴖotes

Chapter 1: Come

[1]"Bless us, O Lord," a translation of "Benedic, Domine," a traditional Catholic prayer before meals dating from the eighth century or before. Author unknown.

[2]"O Come, O Come, Emmanuel," 1851, John Neale's translation of the twelfth-century Latin Advent hymn "Veni, veni, Emmanuel"; Charles Wesley, "Come, Thou Long Expected Jesus," 1744, Isaac Watts, "Joy to the World, the Lord Is Come!" 1719.

Chapter 2: The First Snow of Winter

[1]Amy Grant and Chris Eaton, "Breath of Heaven (Mary's Song)," Home for Christmas (A&M Records, 1992).

[2]"O Come, O Come, Emmanuel," 1851, John Neale's translation of the twelfth-century Latin Advent hymn "Veni, veni, Emmanuel."

[3]William Dix, "What Child Is This?" 1865.

[4]Aristotle, Poetics (650 B.C.).

Chapter 3: Advent

[1]Bing Crosby, White Christmas (MCA, 1986). Original recording titled Merry Christmas (Decca, 1945).

[2]Pueri Cantores of Merano, Christmas in Europe, conducted by Luigi Quaresima (Delta, 1989).

[3]Amy Grant, Home for Christmas (A&M, 1992).

[4]Heinrich Seuse, "In dulci jubilo," 1325.

[5]Johnny Marks, "Rockin' Around the Christmas Tree" (Decca, 1958).

[6]John F. Wade, "Adeste fideles," 1743, trans. Frederick Oakeley, "O Come, All Ye Faithful," 1841.

[7]*How the Grinch Stole Christmas*, dir. Chuck Jones and Ben Washam (MGM, 1966). Based on Dr. Seuss, *How the Grinch Stole Christmas* (New York: Random, 1957).

[8]John Hughes, *Home Alone*, dir. Chris Columbus (20th Century Fox, 1990).

[9]*A Charlie Brown Christmas*, dir. Bill Melendez (Mendelson/Melendez, 1965).

[10]Clement Clarke Moore, "A Visit from St. Nicholas," in *Treasury of Christmas Stories*, ed. Ann McGovern (New York: Scholastic, 1960); the poem is also known as "'Twas the Night Before Christmas," originally published in 1844.

[11]Laura Ingalls Wilder, "Mr. Edwards Meets Santa Claus," in *Treasury of Christmas Stories*, ed. Ann McGovern (New York: Scholastic, 1960). Excerpted from *Little House on the Prairie* (New York: Harper, 1935).

[12]Maud Lindsay, "The Jar of Rosemary," in *Treasury of Christmas Stories*, ed. Ann McGovern (New York: Scholastic, 1960).

[13]W. D. Howells, "Christmas Every Day," in *Treasury of Christmas Stories*, ed. Ann McGovern (New York: Scholastic, 1960).

[14]Lincoln Steffens, "A Miserable, Merry Christmas," in *Treasury of Christmas Stories*, ed. Ann McGovern (New York: Scholastic, 1960).

[15]Anne Wood, "Secret in the Barn," in *Treasury of Christmas Stories*, ed. Ann McGovern (New York: Scholastic, 1960).

Chapter 4: The Faith of a Child

[1]John Gilmary Shea, *Little Pictorial Lives of Saints*, 1878.

[2] Robert Lowry, "Up from the Grave He Arose," 1874.

[3] Fanny J. Crosby (lyrics) and William J. Kirkpatrick (music), "Redeemed by the Blood of the Lamb," 1882.

Chapter 5: "Stille Nacht"

[1] Carrie Oliver, *Journal of Hope*, August 23, 2005 <www.carrieshealth.com>.

[2] Rainer Maria Rilke, "Herbsttag," in *Das Buch der Bilder*, 1902.

[3] Marjorie Holmes, *Two from Galilee: The Story of Mary and Joseph* (Old Tappan, N.J.: Revell, 1972).

Chapter 7: And He Is in the Manger Now

[1] Ben Jonson, "To the Memory of My Beloved, the Author Mr. William Shakespeare: And What He Hath Left Us," *First Folio of Mr. William Shakespeares Comedies, Histories, & Tragedies* (London: William and Isaac Jaggard and Edward Blount, 1623).

[2] Die gantze Heilige Schrift [The entire holy Scriptures], trans. Martin Luther, 1545.

Chapter 8: Anointed

[1] Sei Shōnagon, *The Pillow Book*, trans. Meredith McKinney (London: Penguin, 2006).

[2] Ibid., p. 28.

[3] Ibid., p. 46.

[4] Ibid., p. 154.

Chapter 9: Troughs

[1] Edmund Spenser, "An Hymne of Heavenly Love," *Fowre Hymnes*, 1596.

[2] Wycliffe's Bible, 1382.

[3] J. R. R. Tolkien, "On Fairy-Stories," in *Essays Presented to Charles Williams*, ed. C. S. Lewis (Oxford: Oxford University Press, 1947).

[4]Jacob and Wilhelm Grimm, "Der alte Großvater und der Enkel" [The old grandfather and the grandson], *Kinder- und Hausmärchen* [*Household Tales*], 1812.

[5]Wycliffe's Bible, 1382.

[6]The Geneva Bible, 1599.

Chapter 10: Washing Socks

[1]"Margery, Serve Well the Black Sow," *Deuteromelia*, ed. Thomas Ravencroft, 1609.

[2]Stephen Foster, "Oh! Susanna," 1848.

[3]Matthew White, "Great Tom Is Cast," *Catch That Catch Can: Or, the Musical Companion,* ed. John Playford, 1667.

[4]Nahum Tate, "Whilst Shepherds Watched Their Flocks by Night," *Tate and Brady's Psalter,* ed. Nahum Tate and Nicholas Brady, 1702. Tune: "Old Winchester," *Este's Psalter,* 1592.

Chapter 11: In the Bleak Midwinter

[1]"Act of Contrition," traditional Catholic prayer for confession, translated from Latin. Date unknown.

[2]Alice Sebold, *Lucky* (New York: Scribner, 1999).

[3]"O Come, O Come, Emmanuel," 1851, John Neale's translation of the twelfth-century Latin Advent hymn "Veni, veni, Emmanuel."

[4]Christina Rossetti, "In the Bleak Midwinter," in *The Poetical Works of Christina Georgina Rossetti*, 1904.

[5]Henry Wadsworth Longfellow, "Christmas Bells," 1864.

[6]Pedro the Lion, "I Heard the Bells on Christmas Day," on *Maybe This Christmas Tree* (Nettwerk, 2004).

[7]Sufjan Stevens, "Sister Winter," on *Songs for Christmas* (Asthmatic Kitty, 2006). Used by permission.

[8]Bing Crosby, "Jingle Bells," on *White Christmas* (MCA, 1986). Original recording titled *Merry Christmas* (Decca, 1945).

[9] Blind Boys of Alabama and Tom Waits, "Go Tell It on the Mountain," on *Go Tell It on the Mountain* (Real World, 2004).

[10] Hugh Martin and Ralph Blane, "Have Yourself a Merry Little Christmas," *Meet Me in St. Louis*, 1943; lyrics altered for Frank Sinatra for *A Jolly Christmas* (Capitol, 1957); James Taylor, "Have Yourself a Merry Little Christmas," on *October Road* (Sony, 2002).

[11] "I Am a Poor Wayfaring Stranger," date unknown, likely early 1800s or before.

[12] Natalie Merchant, "Poor Wayfaring Stranger," on *The House Carpenter's Daughter* (Myth America, 2003).

Chapter 12: Seeking God

[1] Flannery O'Connor, "A Good Man Is Hard to Find," in *The Complete Stories* (New York: Farrar, Straus and Giroux, 1971), pp. 117-33.

[2] Herodotus *Histories*, book 1, trans. George Rawlinson (New York: Tudor, 1956), p. 54.

[3] Wycliffe's Bible, 1382.

[4] The Amplified Bible, Lockman Foundation, 1987.

[5] *Hoffnung für Alle: Die Bibel*, International Bible Society (Basel: Brunnen, 2002).

[6] William Tyndale, Newe Testament, 1526.

[7] Lancelot Andrewes, "Sermon 15 Of the Nativitie: Christmas 1622," *Sermons*, ed. G. M. Story (Oxford: Clarendon, 1967), pp. 98-118.

[8] Davidson R. Morse, "Lancelot Andrewes' Doctrine of the Incarnation" (master of theological studies thesis, Nashotah House, 2003), p. 11.

[9] John F. Wade, "Adeste fideles," 1743, trans. Frederick Oakeley, "O Come, All Ye Faithful," 1841.